handwritten: 2020

handwritten: John & Evelyn

Halifax and Me *handwritten: XOXO*

Harry Bruce

Pottersfield Press
Lawrencetown Beach, Nova Scotia, Canada

Library and Archives Canada Cataloguing in Publication

Title: Halifax and me / Harry Bruce.
Names: Bruce, Harry, 1934- author.
Identifiers: Canadiana (print) 20200279041 | Canadiana (ebook) 20200279459 | ISBN 9781989725177 (softcover) | ISBN 9781989725184 (EPUB)
Subjects: LCSH: Bruce, Harry, 1934- | CSH: Authors, Canadian (English)—20th century—Biography. | LCSH: Halifax (N.S.)—Biography. | LCGFT: Autobiographies.
Classification: LCC PS8553.R73 Z46 2020 | DDC C818/.5409—d 23

Author photo: Annabel Bruce

Cover design: Gail LeBlanc

Pottersfield Press gratefully acknowledges the financial support of the Government of Canada for our publishing activities. We also acknowledge the support of the Canada Council for the Arts and the Province of Nova Scotia which has assisted us to develop and promote our creative industries for the benefit of all Nova Scotians.

Pottersfield Press
248 Leslie Road
East Lawrencetown, Nova Scotia, Canada, B2Z 1T4
Website: www.PottersfieldPress.com
To order, phone 1-800-NIMBUS9 (1-800-646-2879) www.nimbus.ns.ca

Printed in Canada

Pottersfield Press is committed to protecting our natural environment. This book is made of material from well-managed FSC®-certified forests and other controlled sources.

Contents

1

In Halifax and Manhattan, Love Conquers All

I owe my life to Halifax, or at least to my parents' having met there in 1927, the age of bathtub rum, the Model T Ford, and plinka-plinka ukuleles. While the city was a historic international seaport, it was also a two-bit provincial capital with a population of only 70,000 at most. It still had blacksmiths, harness-makers and livery stables, but cars and trucks, sold by seventeen auto dealers and repaired by ten service stations, now dominated traffic. Supermarkets had yet to be invented but, no worries, Halifax boasted more than 270 grocery stores. It also had seventy-seven dressmakers, fifty-one butchers, fifteen fish shops, four daily newspapers, countless bootleggers and speakeasies, and luxury steamships that offered romantic cruises to the West Indies. But for lovers like Charles Tory Bruce, twenty-one, and Gladys Agnes King, twenty-two, a moonlit cruise by rented canoe on the Northwest Arm was more than romantic enough.

She had come by train from a posh neigh- bourhood in the distant and exotic Vancouver. With a BA from the University of British Columbia, she was now studying at Dalhousie for her MA in English, and lived in the women's residence, Shirreff Hall. Older than the undergraduates there, she was more opinionated, independent, and daring. She knew the taste of rye whisky. Charlie was from a farm no more distant and exotic than Guysborough County. Fresh from Mount Allison with his BA, he was the greenest reporter at the *Halifax Morning Chronicle*.

Their backgrounds were so wildly different their marrying suggested young love really does conquer all. Though Agnes's father, Harry Wyeth DeWolfe King, was a Nova Scotian, he was not a Charlie Bruce kind of Nova Scotian. Harry's grandfather, the Rev. William Cosell King, earned an MA at Oxford, was presented to King William III, arrived in Nova Scotia in 1797, and became rector of Christ Church in Windsor, principal of the University of King's College there, and chaplain to the local complement of British troops. He was a member of Nova Scotia's Anglican elite, and his son, Harry's father, was director of prisons for the province. Harry, a handsome fellow with a Dick Tracy chin, graduated from Dalhousie Law School in the late 1890s, promptly moved to Vancouver, and married Sadie Caldwell, a descendant of rich Bostonians, and the future mother of my mother.

Charlie's father was William Henry Bruce, and there was nothing elite about him. He was a great- great-grandson of James Bruce, a hard-up Scot who arrived on the north coast of Chedabucto Bay in the 1790s, met and married Catherine Cadell, and in 1805, while helping construct a schoolhouse, died under a falling tree. Their son, Richard Harvey Bruce, fathered Charles Joseph Bruce, who fathered William.

These Bruces were true horny-handed sons of toil. With the help of their wives, children, neighbours, hand tools, and horses, they did the endless, sweaty, gruelling work of turning forests into fields, and cultivating land that seemed to grow stones better than food. They built their own houses, barns, and boats, hauled fish from the bay, and did a bit of lumbering, blacksmithing, and whatever else they had to do simply to survive where they were. When Charlie was twelve, Will solemnly assured him, "Don't worry. You won't have to stay here and spend your life at this kind of work."

Will's wife was Sarah Jane Tory, a farmer's daughter and schoolteacher from a mile or so northwest of the Bruce homestead. A strong-willed and devout Methodist who lived to be ninety-nine, she and Will had four daughters before Charlie. By far the youngest child, he was "the little prince" of the family. His oldest sister Bessie, an unmarried teacher of thirty-two when he entered university, helped pay for his education there.

Excruciating shyness afflicted him at first, but by the time he graduated as valedictorian, Mount A's 260-odd students all knew him not only as a star intercollegiate debater and editor-in-chief of the campus newspaper, but as a published poet. They nicknamed him "the bard," and his reputation as a promising poet spread beyond the campus.

Once in Halifax, he joined The Song Fishermen, a literary club that included him in its publishing of poetry by Maritimers. The most famous were Charles G.D. Roberts, "The Father of Canadian Poetry," and the internationally acclaimed Bliss Carman. It was in Halifax that Charlie wrote *Tomorrow's Tide* (1932), the first of his four collections of poetry handled by national publishers, and the first to earn favourable attention from as far away as the *New York Herald Tribune*. Echoes of the Halifax he knew could be heard nineteen years later in *The Mulgrave Road*, winner of the Governor General's Award for Poetry.

While not a poet, Agnes was a lover of poetry. When I was a teenager and she in her forties, she sometimes burst into an emotional recital of her favourite lines from Carman's verse. Back at Dalhousie, however, it was the sensationally romantic American poet Edna St. Vincent Millay that she chose to write her thesis about.

Millay was the rarest of phenomena: a versifier as celebrated as a Hollywood star. If the extravagant praise that critics heaped upon her work fed her fame, so did her beauty, braggadocio, dramatic public readings, bisexual conquests, and flaunting the joys and virtues of free love. As early as her second collection, one biographer wrote, she was "the unrivaled embodiment of sex appeal, the It-girl of the hour, the Miss America of 1920. It seemed there was hardly a literate young person in all the English-speaking world who was not soon repeating her verses."

Agnes began her thesis by citing Thomas Hardy's opinion that the U.S. had only two great attractions: the skyscraper and the poetry of Millay. She then reported a critic's description of Millay as "petite, blithe and winsome, with appealing greenish-hazel eyes and wondrously lovely auburn hair, dainty, fascinating and adorable, radiating personality so delightful." Agnes herself had wondrously lovely auburn hair, which fell all the way down her back, and Charlie certainly found her fascinating and adorable. Half a century later, a wheelchair-bound Halifax woman, while remembering friends from the summer of '27, told me, "We all loved Charlie. We just adored him, and then that Agnes King came in from Vancouver, and stole him away from us."

The theft, however, was not complete until 1928 in New York City. In January, Canadian Press, the national news agency that had hired Charlie for its Halifax bureau, transferred him to New York. That was the year the Yankees, with Babe Ruth leading "Murderers' Row," won their third straight World Series. *The Lights of New York*, a cheesy gangster movie but the first real talkie, opened at the Strand on Times Square; the Graf Zepppelin glided over the city's skyscrapers; and *Show Boat*, the greatest of all Broadway musicals, continued its run of 572 consecutive performances. Not a bad year to be still only twenty-one, and alone in Manhattan with a good job.

Charlie would later scribble down memories of sharing with a student an apartment on West 13th Street, watching the newly born New York Rangers in action at Madison Square Garden, downing fifty-cent chicken-á-la-king on toast in a greasy spoon at 50th and 7th, and wearing a tuxedo in the gallery while watching a production at Broadway star Eva Gallienne's pioneering repertory theatre on West 14th.

With Prohibition at its peak, he knew a clandestine drinking joint at the rear of an Italian restaurant, and apparently visited that jazziest and most celebrated of all speakeasies, the Cotton Club in Harlem. For excitement, however, nothing matched the arrival in town of Agnes King.

Once she'd collected her MA in May, she showed up in New York, settled in with relatives, and went to work for Bell Telephone. During the three hottest months in Manhattan, she and Charlie dated constantly. They grew closer and closer but then on September 15, CP yanked Charlie back to Halifax. The longer they were apart, the more frantic he grew to see her again. Ending a poem called "Caution," he pitied a young lover who obeyed his elders' warnings not to let his love make him reckless: "He was advised; he stood aside too long/When Love went by."

Refusing to let love go by, Charlie took a train to Yarmouth, caught a steamship to Boston, boarded another train for New York, met Agnes, and asked her to marry him. While it took him two days and a night to get there, and just as long to return, the journey paid off. Agnes had doubted if she loved him quite enough to marry him but Charlie, while with her once again, was so beseeching and determined she could not say no. On December 13, they married. Neither was a devout Christian, but perhaps as a concession to her family's history as Anglicans, they chose for the ceremony the chapel at All Saints Cathedral in downtown Halifax.

Their first home was one of three apartments at 115 Victoria Road, an easy walk from Charlie's job. He was night editor at CP, and five nights a week reported for work on the fourth floor of the six-storey Roy Building on Barrington Street. In 2014, news would break that the Roy, now 120 years old and rotten, would soon give way to a gleaming new tower of more than twenty floors, full of shops, restaurants, offices, and luxury condos.

Once upon a time, Jane Taber reported in *The Globe and Mail*, the old building boasted "about 80 small businesses, paying around $850 month-to-month for heat, light and the ambience – each with its own frosted glass and oak door, like in an old Bogart movie." One former tenant, filmmaker Geoff D'Eon, remembered, "Everbody felt like a private dick. It was a character building full of characters. Each floor had a different vibe." During the five years my father worked there, he went in and out of one of those oak doors thousands of times, and half a century later my wife Penny, while working for the weekly *Barometer*, used another one hundreds of times. Bye-bye, Roy Building.

In 1932, Charlie and Agnes moved a stone's throw from their apartment on Victoria Road to one on Tower Road. Here, for the first time, they had their very own telephone, number B4753. Their son Alan was born in October and, in September 1933, CP transferred Charlie to its head office in Toronto. The second of their four children, all sons, I was born up there on July 8, 1934, but it was here in Halifax that I would spend most of my life.

In early March, 1944, Charlie left Toronto to reach what he would later describe in the narrative poem "Grey Ship Moving" (1945) as "the long seawall at Halifax." Lying there "with her iron troopdecks ready and cold" was the grey ship. The speedy *Andes*, she was built in Belfast from 1937 to 1939 as the Royal Mail Lines' flagship, and designed to carry 607 passengers on luxurious voyages between Southampton and South America. Even before her maiden voyage, however, the Admiralty grabbed her and, stripping her of every trace of splendour, turned her into a bare-bones carrier of up to four thousand troops per voyage. It was thus among thousands of military personnel that war correspondent Charles Bruce, ranked as a captain by the Canadian Army, now boarded the *Andes* for a blessedly uneventful voyage across the North Atlantic to England. The war saw nearly 400,000 military personnel sail for service overseas from the long seawall at Halifax.

CP had named Charlie superintendent of its London bureau, with a staff that included four editors, a troopships reporter, and a changing roster of correspondents covering the Canadian forces in Europe. The bureau edited and relayed back to homeland newspapers the despatches that the correspondents sent about the Canadian participation in the bloody D-Day landings of June 6, 1944, and the combat in western Europe that, over the next eleven more months, helped drive Nazi Germany to its unconditional surrender on May 8, 1945. Three days after the D-Day landings, Charlie told Gillis Purcell, boss of CP, that ever since three days before the landings, "We've been manning the office twenty-four hours a day ... I'm getting in at 9-10 a.m., and trying to get out by midnight."

The following September, high over enemy-held Dutch territory, he endured something far worse than exhaustion. After six months tied to a desk job in London, he felt like the young soldier aboard the

"Grey Ship Moving" who, while struggling to explain why he'd joined up, finally says, "You can't stay out of the show." Charlie hitched a ride on a mission by a Lancaster bomber to drop supplies to Allied forces in Holland and, he later reported, the four-engine "P for Peter" flew "through a literal hell of flak" to reach the drop zone. Mission completed, the pilot turned the big plane for home, but "Then the flak slammed into us ... with the force of a giant fist. For a split second, the aircraft seemed steady on course. Then she went into a screaming nosedive."

After twenty-four hours, word of the crew's fate had still not reached London. At best, it seemed, Charlie was in a Nazi prison camp. At worst, he was dead. I was ten, in grade six, and during the morning recess at my school on Friday, September 22, 1944, I sat on cinders with my back to a wooden fence, and let the tears stream down my cheeks. But I bawled too soon. The pilot regained control of P for Peter, muscled it into unoccupied Belgium, and made an expert belly-landing. Owing to wartime disruptions of communications, neither his message to his home base nor Charlie's to his London office reached its destination until everyone who'd crossed the channel on the Lancaster was already back in England. On Saturday morning, the news of Charlie's "return from the dead" hit front pages across Canada.

"I hope you are feeling fine after your little bit of confusion over Holland," I wrote to him two weeks later. "I bet you were pretty scared when you went into that nose-dive." I then told him about Pal, Sadie, and Conrad, the dogs at a farmhouse near the log cabin at Sand Lake, just north of Huntsville, Ontario, where our family, minus him this time, had recently spent our fourth summer holidays; the swimming lessons that Alan and I were taking in the city from "some German guy called Vercota" (immigrant Ernst Vierkoetter, a burly baker's son from Cologne and world-famous marathon swimmer); and the chest-deep trench that my friend Billy and I had dug, and covered with boards and earth, "so now we have a little underground fort. Good-by for now. Yours Truly, Harry."

During the sixteen months of war that kept Charlie on the far side of the Atlantic, I also sent him such vital information as "I got 76 out of 100 in arithmetic and Alan only got 74, not bad, eh? We're taking up Livingstone. You know, that guy in Africa." After Christmas, 1944, I filed even hotter news: "Alan got me a super comic book and I got him the book *Bob, Son of Battle*. Andy [my younger brother] got me a nice fountain pen, and I got him a Mountie book. I got Mom an apron."

Charlie, in return, dutifully sent me letters every few weeks. He reported that he'd bought lunch for the pilot whose belly-landing had saved his life; that the Germans were hitting London with flying "buzz bombs" or "doodlebugs," which the English dismissed as merely "unpleasant"; and an army officer he knew who, after being pinned down for hours in the wreckage of a bomb-blasted dugout, had escaped with barely a scratch. He told me about the poor heating he endured in the fourth-storey walk-up he rented in Earl's Court; the married couples riding along London streets on tandem bicycles with "a sidecar for the baby"; his playing tennis with other war correspondents in Regent's Park; and in mid-February, of all months, "little yellow flowers popping up in Hyde Park with lots of people and dogs enjoying sunny weather."

I'm sure he wrote to my brothers as often as to me and, looking back, it strikes me he was more affectionate with us while 3,500 miles away in London than while sitting at the family dinner table in Toronto. Throughout our lives as older boys and teenagers, he was less encouraging and talkative than other fathers. It was as though he saw words as too valuable to waste on the likes of us. I was an adult before we were comfortable talking to each other.

2

Unable-bodied Seaman Learns a Few Ropes

In April 1953, two decades after my parents left Halifax, I arrived there for the first time. I was eighteen, and on assignment from the Royal Canadian Navy. Charlie may not have been chummy, but he knew his fatherly duties and somehow managed to pay for Alan and me to earn BAs at his alma mater, Mount Allison University in Sackville, New Brunswick. There, I quickly learned that if I joined the University Naval Training Division (UNTD) for future reserve officers I would have to endure lectures and evening parade drills on campus but then, as a full-time cadet all summer, I'd not only pocket a fat salary at HMCS Stadacona in Halifax but, along with my sea-going pals, sail away to revel in the sinful offerings of exotic ports and great cities. Yes, the word was out. Devilishly handsome in our officers' uniforms, we'd find ourselves free as birds on the streets of London, Paris, Amsterdam, or

Barcelona. Surely, I'd lose my virginity, and what finer way could there be to serve queen and country?

Did I say "queen"? After we'd received our trim black uniforms, complete with gold frills that bore the royal coat of arms, and finished much of our boring on-campus training, we got dismal news. Come summer, the crowning of Elizabeth II would keep so many RCN ships so busy for so long at the Coronation Fleet Review off Portsmouth that we apprentice officers – regarded by real sailors in the RCN as the most babied dimwits in the service – would have to settle for a cruise to Bermuda. Oh, well, that didn't sound so bad, but by late spring it had become a round trip to Sept-Îles, Québec. Yup, join the navy and see the world.

In early April, our little band of cadets, still teenagers and excited to be wearing in public real uniforms of one of Canada's armed forces, climbed aboard a CN train for a quick trip to Halifax. Just as the train pulled out after stopping at Truro, two new passengers, old enough to be our mothers, pushed their way past us with their luggage. Mostly skinny kids with hoarse or piping voices, we were lolling all over the passenger seats and giggling and jabbering away, and those of us who'd sneaked beer aboard in Sackville were a bit tipsy. Cold War tension was rarely far from Canadian minds in 1953, and as one mother looked us over, she said to the other, "God help us if the Russians come!"

If they were typically thrifty Bluenose mothers, they'd also have been disgusted by the navy's blowing taxpayers' money to send us all the way to Halifax for an expensive lunch and to enable a military tailor to measure us for extra uniforms. The lunch was at Stadacona, in the wardroom officers' mess at Admiralty House (now the Naval Museum of Halifax), and nowhere in Canada could we have inhaled a stronger dose of the traditions and glories of the Royal Navy. Built as a Georgian-style mansion overlooking the naval yard and opened in 1819, Admiralty House was big enough to welcome six hundred guests to a ball in 1848. Before the Royal Navy left Halifax for good in 1905, this was the palatial home of thirty-six consecutive admirals, all of them commanders-in-chief of the North American Station.

So here we all are in 1953, striplings who don't yet know a bight from a bollard, and we're surrounded by the ghosts of heroes who fought under Lord Nelson and helped burn down Washington, and we're using sterling silver cutlery and fine china on white linen to eat a scrumptious lunch while chatting with our hosts. They are unexpectedly charming officers of the Royal Canadian Navy, but throughout the summer that follows we will not once see their likes again.

As a candidate for military service, I was less than ideal. I was romantic, sensitive. I secretly wrote poems. I was as skinny as a fencepost, nervous as a cat, shy as a fawn, randy as a goat. I was more doveish than hawkish but, luckily for me that summer, the fiercest battle I endured was the conflict between the allure of mysterious Halifax and my homesickness for Toronto.

Upon visiting Toronto for the first time, New-foundland writer Ray Guy, who'd been inhaling wind straight off the Atlantic all his life, said it smelled of warm mud and soap. Exactly. Mud, soap, and, for me, the moistness in millions of young leaves in early May, the fresh water that sloshed past the dinghy I sailed on Lake Ontario, and the skin of certain girls. Since I hadn't been home since Christmas, my having signed up for the untender mercies of Stadacona until September meant that, for the first time in my life, I'd be away for eight months.

Halifax was not widely known as a place where good times were had by all. During World War II, which had ended only eight years before, a British admiral called it "the most important port in the world," but it was also the most detested city in Canadian history. Floods of war workers and servicemen, along with their sweethearts and families, nearly doubled the population. Seemingly overnight, Halifax became desperately overcrowded, overpriced, underserviced, and undersupplied.

Nowhere could a soldier, sailor, or anyone else find a legal bar or tavern. Gouging landlords, greedy merchants, jam-packed streetcars, and having to line up for hours outside restaurants and movie theatres strained relations between the hordes of newcomers and long-time locals. Finally, during the VE-Day Riots of June 7-8, 1945, thousands of servicemen, mostly sailors, joined by prostitutes and thuggish civilians, broke into liquor and beer stores, helped themselves, and ran wild throughout the downtown. They looted 207 shops, altogether damaged 564 businesses, and generally disgusted and horrified all of respectable Halifax.

Once here for the summer, I began to see it as mysteriously depressing. The clammy mist that often enshrouded it felt like a lingering cloud of the past homesickness of the uprooted, past yearnings of lonely sailors, and past fears of soldiers bound for God knew what in Europe. But if Halifax was gloomy, it was also dramatic. For it had the sea, and all the stories, ships, tugs, horns, toots, whistles, harbour lights, and fogs, tides, and roaring winds that went with the sea. What awaited me in the strange streets of this world port? In what manly adventures would I excel while sailing o'er the bounding main? I was eighteen, and on my way. Halifax was my oyster.

Even a week after unpacking my RCN duffel bag in the UNTD barracks at "Stad," I cheerfully expected a summer-long immersion in the romance of naval history. A bunch of us received a curious assignment. We each had to write a few paragraphs about an imaginary departure from Halifax of RCN ships. Mine began much like this: "As the early morning sun throws shafts of golden light into the grey mist that smothers one of the world's great harbours, there silently emerge the knifing prows and then the long sleek hulls of three superb warships of Her Majesty's Royal Canadian Navy. They are bound for the open yet forever unknowable Atlantic Ocean and, come what may – yes, come what may – they will do their job."

A commissioned officer might have fully appreciated the beauty of my powerful literary work, but it was a coarse petty officer who collected and read the papers. He'd been doing this every May for years and, even before reading ours, said he knew what was in them. "Yeah," he sneered, "the sun's golden rays they're lightin' up all that grey mornin' mist, and here come them mighty streamlined Royal Canadian Navy ships, and they're headin' out to these unknown dangers in the bloody ocean, right? And never say die, blah, blah, blah." That was so close to what each of us had written that a nervous giggle spread among us.

I blushed, and began to wonder if a few bad moments might punctuate the bliss of the coming summer after all. They did.

The most humiliating followed a parade in which all the UNTDs from Ontario, Québec, Newfoundland, and the Maritimes showed downtown Halifax how to march like drunken penguins. I've always blamed the music for this fiasco. Leading us south to Sackville Street then up to the Garrison Grounds, a handful of our pipers set a certain beat, but somewhere aft a brass band pumped out another.

I know how pathetic this excuse sounds but, for whatever reason, we all skipped, paused, skipped again, rushed, lagged, put our left foot in and put our left foot out, and never once put either foot in or out all at the same time. Remember that feeble joke? Watching soldiers on parade, a proud granny says, "Look at that. Everyone's out of step but my Johnny." Well that's what we were, hundreds of future officers of the senior service, and every last one of us a Johnny.

The parade over, we were marched to a cavernous drill hall, and there we stood while a naval officer blasted us with the most filthy and inventive insults I have ever heard. Never before had he seen such a nauseating disgrace to the Royal Canadian Navy as our parade performance. He had a monstrous voice. Using no PA system, microphone, or megaphone he made every disgusting syllable of his obscenities sting clearly in the ears of even us scumbags in the farthest corners of the hall. The harder he found it to come up with fresh insults vile enough to suit us, the more furious he grew. Finally, he could no longer bear even a second more of our stench, and stormed out of our lives. Sixty-seven years later, I remember how deeply ashamed he made me feel.

A fellow Mount Allisonian who, unlike me, completed the three-year UNTD program to become a reserve officer tells me our beastly critic must have been Commander George M. "Trigger" Wadds. Leather-tough, long-seasoned by the navy, and notorious for his salty language, he was boss of the gunnery school at Stadacona and soon to be skipper of the first real warship built in Canada, the destroyer HMCS *Micmac*. The coat of arms on our officers' caps declared "*Dieu et mon droit*," and it was perhaps typical of Wadds's humour that he insisted this meant not "God and my right," as in the ancient divine right of kings, but "Fuck you, Jack, I'm inboard." A loose translation: I'm safely aboard, so forget those poor bastards still in the ocean.

From officers like Wadds down to hard-handed able seamen, those who'd committed their working lives to careers in the navy tended to see us college-boy cadets as contemptible, or at least ludicrous. If the kindest epithet for us was "Untidies," the unkindest was the plural of the acronym for Canadian University Naval Training Division. Seamen were under orders to salute the coat of arms on the cap of any UNTD youth they passed on a Halifax street but most couldn't be bothered. Others saluted smirkingly, at the last possible second, and only if the cadet had a girl on his right arm. Frantically returning the salute, you'd have to rip the arm free and hurl your hand up to your head.

But it was six hundred nautical miles from Halifax that one sailor punished me with a far worse practical joke. During our one training cruise, the 92-metre frigate HMCS *La Hulloise* had brought us to Sept-Îles,

Québec. A small, remote, French-speaking port on the north shore of the St. Lawrence, it was notable for iron companies and their exports but not for the fun it offered English-speaking boys on the loose from a warship. As *La Hulloise* lay at anchor far out in the harbour, a motor launch took us to town in bunches to spend hours of utterly unmemorable shore leave. During one ferrying, it was my job to impress the locals with my own little demonstration of military precision.

Everyone else aboard remained comfortably seated but I stood at the bow facing forward. A whistling wind blasted my face and bashed the boat around, but I was under orders to keep my balance, and pose as straight as a pine mast, with my arms spread above my head to hold horizontal a pole with a boathook on one end. Here comes the Royal Canadian Navy, folks. Once we reached the dock, I would extend the boathook pole to snag a fitting and smartly pull the bow in. This task looked easy but, with a bunch of curious locals looking on, I repeatedly bungled it. The launch kept bucking like a wild horse in a rodeo ring and, when I did hook the fitting, it ducked away with such force I couldn't keep my grip on the pole.

Since releasing it to plop in the water, or just to stick in the fitting and jut in the air, would surely have been an unspeakable disgrace, I had to unhook it, wait for the launch to return near the dock, and then rehook it. Desperate to prove that I, a uniformed member of the Royal Canadian Navy, could handle such a simple task inside a safe harbour, I endured this bucking torture again and again and again. Finally, when I felt my arm might pull loose from its socket, I overheard one sailor behind me say to another, the one handling the boat's motor, that maybe it was time to "give the kid a chance." Now I knew. The moment I'd completed each hooking, the sadist at the motor had switched it into reverse. Did I deserve this? Well, wasn't I the day's most noticeable UNTD dork?

Unlike the war years, Halifax now had fourteen taverns, but they were off-limits to us UNTDs. This lowered both the odds we would disgrace ourselves and our uniforms and the likelihood that beer-fuelled sailors would beat the crap out of us. Knowing, however, that, despite twenty-one being the minimum legal age for drinkers, some tavern waiters tended to serve any guy in a uniform, a few of us broke the rule.

One evening, I sneaked into the Lord Nelson Tavern, ordered a couple of drafts or three, sprinkled them with salt, and downed them with pickled eggs, like a real man. Having peed in the gents' room, I turned to face a beefy, middle-aged RCN officer. His face too close to mine, he said, "Son, you get your arse out of here. RIGHT NOW!" Without even a farewell glance at my unfinished glass of beer, I got my arse out to Spring Garden Road.

Drinking beer on the base on one particular night, however, was not only allowed but seemingly compulsory. We were ordered to compete in the navy's version of chug-a-lug. In parallel lines of a dozen or so, we sat with our bums on the floor and a full glass of beer beside each one of us. At "Go!" the front guy guzzled his beer as fast he could and, at the instant he banged his empty glass down on the floor, the second guy guzzled his beer and, at the instant he ... and so on down the line. The team to finish first won the round.

I can't recall how many rounds followed before

the naming of the champion, but certainly enough to make every last boy half drunk. Then, having endured the enormous pressure of the competition, we were rewarded with the chance to hang around chatting, smoking, and drinking more free beer until we were fully drunk.

Chug-a-lug night had a disgusting aftermath for one of the eight of us who slept in double-bunk beds in a room in a big wooden barracks. He was a tall, blond, athletic, and innocent-looking non-smoker and, like most of my roommates, a good-natured guy from Queen's University. Never in his life had he downed an alcoholic drink, but he always joined his Queen's buddies when they burst into "Come landlord fill the flowing bowl until it doth run over ... For tonight we'll merry, merry be ... Tomorrow we'll be sober."

Obeying orders he chug-a-lugged with the best of us, but then joined the gang relaxing over more beer and, after the bar closed, stayed behind to swallow the leavings in the glasses of those who'd left for the night. Cigarette butts floated in some. I slept in the bunk above him, and, as I climbed down in the morning, had to be careful where I set my feet. Going to bed, he had neatly laid out his uniform on the floor beside him but, sometime in the night, groggily sensed he was about to throw up. Sticking his head out over the floor, he vomited, and went back to sleep. So there lay his uniform, splattered with his spew – and soggy bits of cigarettes.

My own drinking habits were scarcely more mature. One weekend when the RCN let us loose, three of my roommates and I rented a cabin at Hubbards Beach. The first evening there, I drank more than my share of the rum we'd brought and, while we walked to a roadside grocery, I roared out marching orders in what I thought was a hilarious imitation of a bullying drill instructor at Stadacona.

Inside the store when I staggered in were three shy girls, one of them the pretty cashier, as well as a massive bald man in his thirties and his pal, a short, bulky, uniformed soldier who took an instant dislike to me. I think he resented my ridiculing any parade commander, my biting the end off a cucumber to show the cashier how funny I was, and my Toronto accent. He'd been in a pack of soldiers from Camp Borden, Ontario, who had clashed in bloody brawls with a teenage gang from Toronto.

Confronting me, he said, "I could show you a thing or two, sonny boy."

Despite weighing about 135 pounds and never in my life having won a fist fight, not even in my short-pants years, I leaned back with my elbows on the counter, sneered at his crotch, and said, "Okay, pull it out." He smashed me in the face.

Amid my squeals of outrage, we stepped outside to square off. My friends watched nervously. The bald guy stood ready to maim anyone who tried to interfere with the beating the soldier intended to give me. In front of this flat-footed lout in army boots, I adopted a professional boxer's stance, and danced around him in the style of Sugar Ray Robinson. He half-heartedly pushed his left fist forward. I blocked it with my right hand, but it felt as heavy as a curling stone. And why was he smiling like that?

Luckily, I never found out. One of my friends stepped up, lied that I'd just drunk the first booze of my life, said the soldier could surely understand it had gone to my head, and got me the hell out of there. Walking back to the cabin, my rescuer said, "You completely outclassed him, Harry. You'd have murdered him."

A week later, we were ordered to watch boxing matches between ratings at a ring in a Stadacona. To launch the first fight, the referee called the combatants to touch gloves at the centre of the ring. One guy was muscular, stocky, and cocky. He looked like he'd been there dozens of times, and why was he smiling like that? The other was younger, taller, skinnier, paler, and trembling. A few seconds later, the short one jolted him with a left jab, then nailed his chin with a right uppercut that snapped his head back so hard I thought his neck might be broken. Down he went, out cold. The RCN had tied a lamb to a stake, and invited a wolf in for dinner.

On my second night at Hubbards, I drank beer in a barn-like building, and watched two gorgeous young women dance together to recorded music. At high school dances in Toronto, a girl only danced with another if no boy had asked her. Either of these two then would surely be breathlessly grateful for a chance to glide around with her body snuggled against mine. Tapping one on a shoulder, I said, "Do you mind if I cut in?" Scarcely missing a beat to laugh in my face, they hugged each other tighter, and danced away. I later saw them kissing mouth to mouth. By comparison with today's eighteen-year-olds, I was absurdly naive but, like the chug-a-lug barfer, I was learning a bit that summer, though not all that much about navigation or torpedoes.

Halifax was still more like the town my parents

had known than the city it is today. Its population had barely reached 100,000, and its biggest buildings were still the Nova Scotian and Lord Nelson hotels. It still had a few blacksmiths, ten coal suppliers, fifteen neighbourhood movie theatres with one screen each, and, in the absence of supermarkets and shopping malls, more than two hundred grocery stores. Older Haligonians remembered the pop song about "Barney Google, with the goo-goo-googly eyes," but otherwise "Google" didn't exist. Nor did the Internet, computers, smartphones, iPads, iPods, Facebook, YouTube, tweets, bots, trolling, Netflix, Amazon, or any of their offspring, siblings, cousins, or rivals. Halifax had yet to see television, for heaven's sake, nor even one bridge to Dartmouth.

Crossing the Northwest Arm, however, was easy and, for me, on the hottest Saturday of 1953, the prelude to a magical afternoon at the Dingle with a young woman I thought I would love forever. To reach it, we joined a half-dozen other passengers aboard a small, open ferry at the foot of Oakland Road, paid the skipper a few nickels and dimes, and sat back while he triggered his outboard motor and nipped across the Arm to drop us near the Sir Sandford Fleming Memorial Tower. (Josiah Boutilier had started the service long before Charlie and Agnes first explored the Arm, and his sons Fred and Foster ran it now.)

We spent the afternoon in bathing suits, lolling close together on the soft sand of the little beach over there and occasionally bouncing around in the water. Not the lakewater I had known in Ontario, but salt water. I could smell it. I could smell her. And the Arm, that fiord without cliffs, that haven for ocean-going sloops, cutters, and ketches, was the most beautiful stretch of water I had ever seen.

But my beloved turned out to be merely one of the half-dozen nubile girls I knew that summer. On nights that my friends and I were confined to our barracks near the southern end of the base, I sometimes pulled on grey flannel trousers, a maroon pullover, and sneakers and scrambled over the high wire fence at North Street to keep a date with the latest love of my life. I'd take her to a movie – classics like *From Here to Eternity*, *Roman Holiday*, and *Shane* were all playing in Halifax – or to The Bill Lynch Show, with its midway, "freaks," cotton candy, Ferris wheel, and scarier rides like the Tilt-O-Whirl and Octopus.

I later climbed back over the wire fence at Stadacona and, as sly as a cat burglar, slunk across the open ground where the twelve-storey Juno Tower for naval officers now stands, and back into the barracks. Around midnight, while the boys from Queen's gently snored, I congratulated myself for having once again flouted military authority, and smugly dozed off.

It was on evenings I was in uniform and legally freed from Stadacona that I first met my consecutive girlfriends, usually at dances with live bands in the YWCA on Barrington Street, the long-gone Jubilee Boat Club on the Arm, now the site of one of the city's priciest condo buildings, and The Olympic Gardens Dance Hall at Hunter and Cunard streets. A community centre these days, it opened in 1948 and boasted a revolving stage. When one band took a break, the stage spun round to let a second take over, and the music never stopped. Nor did the illicit boozing at tables on the balcony that surrounded the whole swinging scene.

In 1950, when online dating services were beyond the wildest speculations of futurists, the *Daily Mail* in the U.K. reported that 70 percent of Britain's married couples had met at dance halls. The girls I knew in my first Halifax summer were mostly only a year or two older than me but, considering my goofiness, probably felt a decade more mature. They went to dances, unaccompanied, at least partly to find future husbands. A couple allowed me into their bed-sitting rooms for enough "heavy petting" to drive me dizzy with fumbling horniness, but gently drew the line at "going all the way." I was an ardent lover with money in my pockets, but still an aimless college boy from Toronto, and good enough only until a more promising prospect showed up. I ended the summer with my virginity intact.

I decided in late August that, due to my sensitivity and artistic temperament, I was unsuited for life under the crude authoritarianism of military service, and resigned from the UNTD. Okay, okay. I was too sissy for the RCN, so I quit. But owing to all that marching around, daily exercising, and eating good meals at the same time every day, I felt fitter than I ever had before, or would again. And even though I disliked Stadacona, the city had remained intriguing all summer.

By the time I left, not knowing if I'd ever return, it had occurred to me that a great old saltwater port like Halifax, no matter how puny as a city, might just have something that a lakeport like Toronto, no matter how gigantic, could never have: a deal with the oceans of the world, and their human history. And now? From the balcony of our eleventh-floor condo near Windsor and North, I see the bridges to Dartmouth, bridges that didn't even exist in 1953; the white ferries, toys at this distance, nipping back and forth on the blue of the harbour; and in the south, the high-rises on the downtown waterfront, skyscraping cranes, the green mound of Citadel Hill; and if I lean far enough over the railing, even a stretch of the open Atlantic. The view reminds me, sixty-seven years after my fling with the navy, that the deal with the oceans was a major reason why I finally came to call Halifax home.

3

Tricks Up the Old Port's Sleeve

For ten years after riding the Ocean Limited home to Toronto, I neither saw Halifax nor let it linger on my mind. I graduated from Mount A in '55, promptly joined *The Ottawa Journal* (which died twenty-five years later) as a cub reporter, turned twenty-one on July 8, and on September 10 married Penny Meadows. I had met her in high school, and she was now nineteen. Owing to a scholarship I landed, we sailed to England in September of 1956, loved London until the spring of '57, and bummed around Europe for two months. By September we were back in Ottawa, and I was back at the *Journal*. That lasted until the summer of '59 when, unaccountably restless, I quit the juicy post in the Parliamentary Press Gallery that the *Journal* had given me and joined *The Globe and Mail* in Toronto as a mere City Hall reporter.

By the spring of '60 I could no longer bear to listen for hours on end – in a stuffy room that had been gathering dust in Toronto's old City Hall since the nineteenth century – to the rancorous and hair-splitting deliberations of the city councillors on the Buildings and Development Committee. As a cause of fatal heart afflictions, workplace boredom now ranks with obesity and heavy smoking, but in those days I knew only that I was enduring cruel and unusual punishment for a crime I couldn't possibly have committed.

I was twenty-five, Penny twenty-four and pregnant with our first child, and we were California dreamin'. From the U.S. consulate in Toronto, we got visas permitting us to work in the land of John Wayne and home of the surfboard. Seated at a desk under a photo of President Eisenhower, the woman who handed them to us looked like a tough old New England schoolmarm. She assured us we'd find "plenty of you Britishers" in California.

We rode coach class by rail from Toronto to Chicago to Los Angeles and then, while I looked for a job, sponged off Penny's older sister Wendy and her husband Vincent. We moved right in with them and their four young daughters at their blossom-fragrant home on Ocean Way in Santa Monica. It was near the towering palms of Palisades Park, up above the stupendous Pacific as it rolled ashore.

Sailing by catamaran, romping in breaking surf, lolling on cushiony sand under sunny skies, exploring lush canyons in Wendy's little black Sunbeam-Talbot convertible (the only "Britisher" I met out there) and, on the night of July 4, marvelling at the most extravagant fireworks I'd ever seen burst above mile after mile of beach, I began to think, yes, this might just be the place to spend the rest of our lives.

But the only newspaper I deigned to consider joining was the *Los Angeles Times* and, although its managing editor agreed to see me, neither my credentials nor manner impressed him. The boss of a big, big-city newspaper, he was Busy. As impatient and formidable as my father, he seemed to think Ottawa and Toronto were little more than Indian villages in the Canadian wilds. I turned timid to the point of incoherence, and how could a shrinking Canadian violet possibly be a hotshot Los Angeles reporter? Did I not know that scores of bold, hustling, and seasoned newshounds, all of them Californians, lusted after jobs on his paper?

By autumn, I was back covering Toronto City Hall for *The Globe*, and listening to the old, familiar yammering at the Buildings and Development Committee. Then, in the summer of '61, I again jumped ship, this time to become a junior editor at *Maclean's* magazine. *Globe* managing editor Richard (Dic) Doyle, who had forgiven me for my disloyal flight to California by re-hiring me, now told a colleague I was "an incurable flitter." He himself was fanatically loyal to *The Globe*, and would excel there as the most tough-minded and influential Canadian newspaper editor of the second half of the twentieth century. About me, he was dead-on.

I flitted in 1964 from *Maclean's* to *Saturday Night* magazine, and from there to *The Canadian Magazine*, *The Star Weekly*, *The Toronto Daily Star*, the federal Task Force on Government Information, and, once again, *Maclean's*. Meanwhile, Penny and I flitted with our children from one address to another in Toronto, and then to a brick house we bought an hour's horrible drive east in the lakeside village of Newcastle, further east to a house we rented in Ottawa, and then in 1970 back to our place in Newcastle.

By then, I had made two short flits in and out of the old port. The first was a full decade after my undistinguished stint at HMCS Stadacona. While ecstatic to be working for *Maclean's* – magazines, I believed, treasured not grubby reporters but writers – I was still the lowliest of editors, a fixer-upper of others' prose. Now, however, I persuaded my superiors that, since I'd spent years in the Maritimes, I was just the fellow to explore and write a national story that I saw unfolding in Halifax.

And that's how it came about that my name appeared in capital letters under the first story on the first page in the *Maclean's* of mid-November 1963. The first sentence of the first paragraph of that lucid and perceptive little masterpiece began like this: "If John Diefenbaker quits the Tory leadership fairly soon, and if the Ontario Tories don't want Manitoba Premier Duff Roblin of Manitoba to replace him, and if the Prairie Tories reject Premier John Robarts of Ontario, and if some darker Tory horse doesn't make a marvelous spurt for the wire, then the next leader of the federal Conservatives will likely be the bony premier of Nova Scotia, Robert L. Stanfield."

To explore this speculation, I had arranged to interview the man himself, and he chose to meet me in his office at Province House on a Saturday morning in late October. The building is the oldest seat of government in all of Canada. Every year since 1819, the legislative assembly of Nova Scotia has gathered there. In 1835, when the colony's Supreme Court was meeting in what's now the legislative library, Province House was where journalist Joseph Howe beat a charge of seditious libel with a passionate and eloquent speech, six hours long, that historians would later recognize as the first step in the establishment of freedom of the press in the future Canada.

Witnessing the opening of the legislature there in early 1842 was none other than Charles Dickens, at twenty-nine already famous on both sides of the Atlantic for having written *The Pickwick Papers*, *Oliver Twist*, *Nicholas Nickleby*, and *The Old Curiosity Shop*. He'd arrived in town aboard the Boston-bound *Britannia*, the pioneering trans-Atlantic paddlewheel steamer built in 1840 by the Halifax-born shipping tycoon, Samuel Cunard. It was Howe, by now both an influential Reform member of the legislature and Speaker of the House, who showed Dickens around the port and into the show at Province House.

While gently mocking the members' political posturing following the Speech from the Throne, Dickens wrote that the whole event was like watching an opening of Parliament at Westminster "through the wrong end of a telescope." At Province House six years later, and owing mostly to Howe's leadership, Nova Scotia became the first colony in the British Empire to achieve responsible government.

Dickens praised the building as "a gem of Georgian architecture," and *The Canadian Encyclopedia* calls it "the most noteworthy example of Palladian architecture in Canada." But despite everything that made Province House memorable, I somehow could not recall in '63 ever having seen it during my romantic and tipsy wanderings in '53. I therefore phoned it from my room at the Nova Scotian Hotel to learn how to get there.

Stanfield himself picked up the phone, but didn't identify himself. He gravely explained, "You just go out the front door of the hotel, turn right on Hollis Street, walk four short blocks north, and on your left you'll see this big, old historic-looking building, three-storeys high, and that's it." And there it was, its Palladian walls sweating history. High on a pedestal on the south lawn stood a bronze Joseph Howe, his right arm extended (to fend off adoring women, joked those who appreciated his immortal reputation as a womanizer).

A white-haired commissionaire met me at the entrance. He appeared to be alone in the building, but guided me down a shadowy hall to a modest office. And there, behind a desk in a sharp grey business suit on this golden and fall-fragrant Saturday morning – when he probably wished he was raking and burning leaves outside his home in the South End – sat the seventeenth premier of Nova Scotia, the lanky, balding Robert L. Stanfield. Having now covered both federal and provincial politics, I knew that never in an eternity of Saturdays would I stroll into the Parliament Buildings and find Prime Minister Lester "Mike" Pearson in his office, or into Queen's Park in Toronto to spend an hour chatting with the formidable Premier John Robarts, known throughout Ontario as "The Chairman of the Board."

Stanfield was friendly enough, but reserved, more professorial than prime ministerial, and without an iota of charisma. I could easily imagine him at

Harvard, where he'd been both an honours student in law and the first Canadian editor of the *Harvard Law Review*, but not as the political wizard who'd led Bluenose Conservatives to three decisive election victories in seven years, the last of them by thirty-nine seats to the Liberals' four.

How could he possibly have done it? He was no Joe Howe on the hustings. His strongest oratorical gift was earnest doggedness, not a quality you'd expect in a potential prime minister. Why then were political circles in Halifax abuzz with the rumour that Stanfield, at forty-nine, had hired a tutor in French? He laughed at the story. He thought English-speaking Canadians probably should learn French, but hadn't studied it himself since his Harvard days.

"So you won't be competing for the top Tory job in the country," I said.

Dodging neatly, he said, "Well, it's always foolish to say you would never do anything. I used to say I would never go into politics at all."

We chatted a bit about the weather. The most disappointing months in Nova Scotia, he confided, were November because winter always arrived sooner than expected and April because it always lingered longer. My editors failed to see such opinions as a scoop worth the expense of having sent me to Halifax, but four years later I at least had the satisfaction of seeing my political hunch finally come true. At a national convention in Ottawa, Stanfield won the Tory leadership on the fifth ballot, and although Pierre Trudeau and the Liberals would beat him and the Conservatives in three consecutive elections, his integrity, political courage, and honourable record in the Commons led to his being remembered as "the best Prime Minister Canada never had."

The Halifax I visited to see him wasn't quite the same as the one I'd known a decade earlier. This time, I was here for only three days, but at the height of the most glorious fall I'd ever seen. Unlike the red-brick Toronto I knew so well, Halifax was mostly a wooden city, and up and down the older residential streets, elegant and brightly painted Victorian houses glowed between great corridors of hardwoods, all adazzle in orange, crimson, yellow, and gold. The harbour was a deeper, sharper blue than I remembered and, high above it now, the sweeping curves of that triumph of modern engineering, the suspension bridge, carried cars and trucks between Halifax and Dartmouth. I was seeing the Angus L. Macdonald Bridge for the first time.

The easy accessibility of the premier on a weekend morning, and his civilized manner, somehow seemed exactly right for the city. Along with the good-natured folks under the magical sunshine in the streets and parks, and the amiable connoisseurs of local beer I met in taverns, Stanfield made me feel as Dickens did upon leaving 121 years earlier: "The day was uncommonly fine, the air bracing and healthful, the whole aspect of the town cheerful, thriving and industrious. I carried away with me a most pleasant impression of the town and its inhabitants."

Seven years passed before I made another return flit to Halifax. I was back at *Maclean's* as a writer-editor, and my pal Peter Gzowski, whom I'd first known as its managing editor in the early '60s, had also returned, but this time as editor-in-chief. He had not yet launched his career as an interviewer on CBC radio for three hours every weekday morning. His warm, persuasive voice, flattering curiosity, and perceptive questions in that job would inspire *Maclean's* to declare, "In the last two decades of the 20th century, Peter Gzowski was as close to a Captain Canada as this country has ever seen."

But in his unfamous days as a magazine man he had not been so lovable. He was a hard-drinking, hard-womanizing, and frequently insulting chain-smoker. At the same time, he was funny, creative, with it, and, for my money, the smartest young editor in all of Canada's print media. His genius, however, must have been in hibernation when he agreed in early March 1970 that I should visit Halifax to interview Canada's most distinguished beer baron, Colonel Sidney Culverwell Oland.

Peter had decided to run a series of stories called "Wisdom." They would star elderly Canadians whose astonishing achievements, adventures, or triumphs over personal disaster had left them with yarns and sagacity that could not help but fascinate hundreds of thousands of younger *Maclean's* readers. I nominated Oland as the perfect golden oldie to launch the series.

An officer in the Canadian Field Artillery during World War I, he had served at the battles of both Passchendaele and Amiens, and earned mentions in despatches signed by none other than Winston Churchill. When Prohibition shut down the family brewery in Halifax in the '20s, Oland set about building a railroad in Jamaica. He also went to work in Hollywood as a technical director for silent movies and, handsome and strapping as he was, an actor as well. What scandals might he finally reveal about, say, Rudolph

Valentino, Mary Pickford, or Clara "The It-Girl" Bow? During the Depression, he revived old gold mines to make work for Nova Scotian miners.

His family had been brewing beer here since before Confederation, and he had himself spent close to four decades as the wily and forceful boss of Oland and Son Limited, the biggest brewer in the Maritimes. He was a multi-millionaire, director of a dozen national companies, and the Bluenose philanthropist par excellence. He and the brewery financially backed construction of the Oland Centre sports complex at St. Francis Xavier University, the founding of Neptune Theatre, and teams, fairs, and exhibitions all over the province. On his Nova Scotia farms, he raised the finest Ayrshire cows and Aberdeen Angus cattle.

Finally, Col. Oland had served as honourary aide-de-camp to no fewer than four Governors General of Canada, and I ask you now, how could such a man not be just brimful of wise advice and great stories? Alas, he had not an ounce of either. Not for me anyway. Either I was too clumsy an interviewer or the good colonel, going on eighty-five, was way past his best-before date. (I should talk. I am now eighty-six.)

We met in his office at Keith Hall. A three-storey edifice of sandstone and brick in the Italianate style, it was built in 1863 by Scottish-born brewmaster Alexander Keith. Now, it was the city's most elegant little office building. On adjoining land that sloped towards the harbour, Keith had founded his brewery in 1819, and the site still boasted a Dickensian assemblage of ironstone and granite buildings around a cobblestone courtyard. Oland's Brewery bought Keith's in 1928, when the colonel was forty-two, and now, after

Prohibition, the Great Depression, World War II, the Booming Fifties, and excessively Swinging Sixties, here he was, boss emeritus of his unsinkable family business, and he had no idea who I was, why I was there, or what to tell me.

But how would I like to look around *Bluenose II* with him? Aah! Now you're talking, Colonel. Unlike him, I couldn't say I was a Chevalier of Merit of the Order of Peru, or a Knight of the Sovereign Military Order of Malta, or a Commander of the Order of St. John of Jerusalem, but we did have one important thing in common. We both loved sailing. He did his aboard this magnificent wooden schooner, half as long as a football field, while I did mine on centreboard dinghies but, what the heck, sailing is sailing, and I could not have imagined a more thrilling late-winter gift than a stroll aboard the beautiful replica of the most famous sailing ship in Canadian history.

The original *Bluenose* was designed and built in Lunenburg both to harvest cod off Newfoundland and to race against comparable schooners from Glouces-ter, Massachusetts. In the '20s and '30s, she proved so triumphant in several series of races that she became not only an immortal source of bragging rights among Nova Scotians but a sea-going celebrity all across Canada.

Years later, my father, stuck in Toronto and deep-ly homesick for life beside the Atlantic, recalled both the excitement the international races had aroused in Halifax when he was a young newsman there and the stories about them that he'd helped Canadian Press speed across country. It wasn't until 1952 that his collec-tion, *The Mulgrave Road*, won the Governor General's

Award for poetry, but one of its poems opened with a tribute to the skippers and crewmen in those long-gone races:

These are the fellows who smell of salt to the prairie,
Keep the back country informed of crumbling swell
That buckles the international course off Halifax
After a night of wind:
Angus Walters and Ben Pine, carrying on for Tommy
Himmelman and Marty Welch,
Heading up the tough men who get into the news,
Heading up the hard men of Lunenburg and Gloucester,
Keeping the cities burdened with grass and grain
Forever mindful that something wet and salt
Creeps and loafs and marches round the continent,
Careless of time, careless of change, obeying the moon.

In 1938, when I turned four, an image of *Bluenose* began to sail close-hauled across the "tails" side of the Canadian dime, and eighty-two years later she's still there. In 1947, when I turned thirteen and first raced dinghies on Toronto harbour, my favourite among the more than1,300 postage stamps I'd collected was an old Canadian one, big and blue, that showed her charging along under full sail, leaving some Yankee loser way back on a distant horizon.

The death of *Bluenose* was ignominious. In 1946, stripped of masts, rigging, and sails, and with engines installed, she was putt-putting around the West Indies as a two-bit coastal freighter when, while laden with bananas, she struck a coral reef off Haiti and broke up. A Halifax daily called this nothing less than "a national shame" and seventeen years later the Oland brewery – with Colonel Sidney its chairman, and his three sons its president and vice-presidents – paid $300,000 ($2.5 million in 2019 currency) for the creation of *Bluenose II.*

For its design, the Olands relied on the original plans for the *Bluenose* and, for its construction, the same shipyard in Lunenburg, and even some of the same skilled workers. The result was a gleaming and glorious resurrection – plank by plank, sail by sail, from stem to gudgeon – of the late and still lamented "Queen of the North Atlantic."

Just as the sun broke through the mist over Lunenburg harbour late one July morning in 1963, the Spanish-born Herlinda deBedia Oland, the colonel's wife for half a century, whacked a champagne bottle on the bow of *Bluenose II* and, as applause erupted from 15,000 spectators, more than four times the port's population, the sleek, black hull slid into the harbour. At a reception in the local community centre, guests would find three dories, packed to the gunwales with ice and bottles of beer, Oland beer.

Since one of the widely beloved Oland brews was already Schooner Lager, *Bluenose II* was an ocean-going beer commercial, both unique and fabulous. No other brewery would ever declare, "I'd sooner have a Schooner" or "The Schooner, the better." But she was also the ultimate family yacht for the colonel and his boys; a bold tribute to the original *Bluenose* and Nova Scotia's high-seas history; and, as both a charter ship for the adventurous and simply a grand sight to behold, a memorable tourist attraction.

Once walking, the colonel seemed spry enough and had no trouble guiding me down through the brewery, across Lower Water Street, and past a few ridges of slush on a long dock. Alongside lay *Bluenose II*. Her skipper escorted us aboard, and just before we went below, an Afro-Canadian deckhand nodded a polite greeting. Seen from a distance, the vessel was a ringer for the first *Bluenose*, but below decks she was definitely something else. She boasted the most up-to-the-minute navigation equipment, two 170-horsepower diesels, luxurious cabins, and a galley where chefs could whip up gourmet dinners even during heavy weather. In the space where the first *Bluenose* jammed tons of dead fish, the second boasted a sumptuous saloon that smelled of oiled teak and the finest leather, and that's where we three sat down to chat.

The colonel opened the discussion.

"Was that a black man I saw aboard the *Bluenose*, captain?"

"I'm afraid it's a bit hard to find good crew this time of year, sir."

"Well, just make damn sure he's gone before the tourist season starts."

"Yes, sir."

That killed the *MacLean's* Wisdom series. News that the most memorable revelation I gained during my time with the colonel was that he was at least somewhat racist rang alarms in Gzowski's head. Yes, Canada had wise old people, but maybe it also had quite a few who were cranky, envy-riddled, grudge-filled, foul-mouthed, puffed-up, or excruciatingly boring. Sorting out the fascinating wheat from the odious chaff would be too much trouble, and who were we anyway to elevate the elderly above the young and middle-aged? Goodbye, Wisdom.

But just before I'd left Halifax, something good

had happened. On one of those freakishly warm days that envelop the city once or twice most winters, I happened to be strolling around in the South End neighbourhood where my parents lived and loved before I was born. Such days smell faintly of future blossoms and, as the snow melts into gurgles in the gutters, sound like busy creeks in May. They can make you giddy, and on Victoria Road three happy guys in their early twenties sat on the front steps of an old wooden house. Their feet were bare, they wore only trousers and singlets under that amazing summer sun, and each had a bottle of Olands. As I passed, they greeted me politely, and even offered me a Schooner lager. I was too startled to accept but, walking on down the street toward the CN tracks and, beyond them, the ancient harbour, I felt curiously high on Halifax.

Now and then, she's a bit of a flirt.

4

Movin' East

Within a year, the colonel and his sons had neither brewery nor *Bluenose II*, and *MacLean's* had neither Gzowski nor me. The Olands in Halifax-Dartmouth had been making and selling beer for well over a century, but in 1971 they sold their breweries to the Ontario-based giant, Labatt Breweries of Canada, and gave their beloved schooner to Nova Scotia as a tool to promote tourism.

And Gzowski and me? Back in '64, the owners of *Maclean's* had so insultingly expressed their contempt for the way editor-in-chief Ken Lefolli was doing his job that he quit, and we two were among the five staff who revered him enough to follow him out the door. Now, for similar reasons, Gzowski quit and, for the second time in seven years, I felt obliged to resign from the magazine where I'd hoped to spend the rest of my working life. Gzowski drifted into his phenomenal career at CBC Radio and I, fed up with aimlessly barging in and out of jobs in Toronto and Ottawa, decided to aimlessly barge in and out of freelance writing beside the Atlantic Ocean.

Throughout the summer of 1946, when I turned twelve, I stayed with a bunch of Bruces at the old family homestead in Port Shoreham, a settlement on a dirt road that flanked the north shore of Chedabucto Bay in Guysborough County. I slept in the tiny second-floor room where my father was born, played nearly every day with the MacIntosh kids from the adjacent farm, and gradually came to love a life as different from the one I knew in Toronto as kerosene lamps were from light bulbs, and outhouses from flush toilets.

To me, at that age, July and August were a year long. As the car that finally carried me away for my rail trip home passed the four young MacIntoshes on the far side of a field, they all waved goodbye, and I burst into tears. I would never forget them, or what my father described in one poem as "the long grumbling sigh of the bay at night." Facing south, the Bruce beach on that bay lies on a strip of gravel and sand that curves between two heads for three miles. Sky, sea, wind, and land all get together there to offer spectacular freedom to sailing gulls, and children on the loose.

In August 1970, twenty-four years after my boyhood adventure down home, Penny and I decided to give Alec, nine, Annabel, eight, and Max, barely two, a taste of what I'd so loved. We loaded our big, tinny Chevy van with five pricey sleeping bags, two greasy tents, two folding chairs, one propane cookstove, pots, pans, tools, Band-Aids, flashlights, and, well, just the whole, great, cumbersome kit for family camping back in the days when gas stations gave away road maps. With the kids bouncing around on mattresses in the cargo space behind the seats – those were also the days before seatbelts – we drove down from our home in Newcastle, Ontario, to experience a week of what I promised would be heavenly tenting on the old Bruce beach.

Behind the beach rose a ten-acre knot of messy forest. Locals had once known it all as "Bruces' Island" but it was actually a peninsula. No one had ever built anything on this gnarled hump of fir, spruce, moss, and wire birch, but it included the family's entire saltwater frontage, more than nine hundred feet of it.

We pitched our tents just above high water, and for four days the sun shone on us from dawn to dusk. A gentle southwesterly stroked us from way across the bay and filled the two tents with movement and soft noises. I discovered the calmness that a peaceful ocean shore offers anyone who cares to lie down just above the surf and wait for a while. I snored in the afternoon. Every morning before breakfast, I took an axe and headed up the hill, knocked down rotten trees, trimmed the lower branches off thick evergreens, and hauled it all down to burn on the beach.

For no good reason, I was clearing a skinny path to the highest part of Bruces' Island. Up there, the gulls wheeled and squawked a few feet above my head, and there was never a time the sound of the surf below did not move with the wind in these high trees. Creating the path was the sweetest kind of work. I sang and talked to myself, and Alec often joined me with his hatchet.

So few people visited the beach that we waded and swam naked, morning and afternoon. At night, we combined driftwood with my forest garbage to build the world's finest bonfires, and eat hotdogs and marshmallows we burned black. Alec and Annabel stayed up late to swim some more. Penny and I sat there past midnight. We poked the dwindling fire, talked quietly under the starlight, drank too much rum, and in the morning – miracle of miracles! – woke up feeling just fine, and I carried my axe back up to the little forest.

And then, during our fifth dawn, the first Nova Scotia hurricane of our lives destroyed heaven. It rampaged across the bay, threatened to rip our tents apart, and, since we'd stupidly pitched them at the bottom of a bare slope, flooded our whole campsite. We frantically dumped all our gear into the van, dragged our soggy arses into the seats, and hit the road for Newcastle. What the hurricane could not drown, however, was the thrill we got from just four days of living beside the ocean. Penny and I now yearned for a chunk of the Nova Scotia coast we could call our own.

I was sure it could not possibly be the Bruce homestead. My aunt Bess, a healthy seventy-nine (whose mother had lived to be ninety-nine), owned it, and two of her younger sisters liked to descend on it in summer. My brothers and first cousins each had as much right to it as I did. Pursuing the homestead might be complicated, and owning it would mean responsibilities we weren't sure we wanted. I asked my father about other possibilities.

When I dropped in on him at the Toronto house where he had lived with my mother and us boys since long before he had packed me off for my summer at the homestead, I was thirty-six and he sixty-four. He was facing east in his favourite stuffed chair and smoking his pipe. We were considering buying land on the Northumberland Strait, I told him, because the water there was fairly warm.

"Oh, sure," he said. "It's fine for swimming over there – if you like muck, eelgrass, and seaweed."

What about the South Shore?

"It's pretty all right, but expensive, just a dormitory for Halifax, really. For rugged beauty, I've always preferred the Eastern Shore."

Should we buy there then?

"Well, you'd certainly get a good deal, if you don't mind fog three days out of four."

He took a drag on his pipe and gazed at the eastern sky.

"Of course, at Port Shoreham, the weather's more like you get in Cape Breton, lots of sunshine." And then, one of the happiest surprises of my life: "You know, you should consider the homestead. We could work something out with Bess, and it wouldn't cost you much."

The edge of the steep bluff at the top of Bruces' Island, he said, was a terrific spot for a cabin. If you felled a few trees up there, you could look eastward and you'd be so high you'd see over Ragged Head and right out to the ocean. You could look down at the backs of birds cruising the surface of the water. You could look across the wide sweep of the bay to the purple and cobalt hills beyond or, at night, the blink-blink of the Queensport lighthouse. He was finding all the right words, and soon persuaded Bess to give us Bruces' Island.

All this was in the back of my mind when, after

playing a decade of musical chairs with employers in Toronto and Ottawa, I said to Penny, "Hey, let's try Halifax!" She agreed, and to gain a small but guaranteed income while I chased freelance work up there while living down here, I bagged a half-time job in public relations at the old Nova Scotia Light and Power Company. By March 28, 1971, only seven months after the hurricane drove us off the beach, we'd sold our house in Newcastle, shipped all our furniture down there, traded the van in on a blue-green Pontiac Strato Chief, put the kids in the back seat with a tiny black kitten, and, in our mid-thirties, set out on the most important journey of our lives.

"You'll have a lot of fun down there," my father had predicted.

While agreeing to hire me, Russell Harrington, the president of the power company, had strongly recommended we look for a house in the Armcrescent neighbourhood. He and his wife lived there quietly, inexpensively, and happily. Though childless, they saw it as the perfect enclave for young families. Just northwest of the Connaught-Quinpool intersection, it was handy to both everyday shopping, and all that the downtown offered. Not only that, it was within the best school district in the city, and its streets bore so little through traffic that youngsters still used them for ball hockey and learning to ride bikes. Parents kept an eye on one another's kids, excelled at gardening, cleared snow from the driveways of the elderly, and got together for yard sales and Christmas parties. Armcrescent really was what real estate agents loved to call "Halifax's best kept secret."

So I promptly placed a hefty down payment on a

new and squeaky clean bungalow sixteen miles away, and by early April we were unpacking, arranging furniture, peering out windows, and just trying to get to know the first home we'd ever had with two bathrooms, unsullied toilets, virgin appliances, immaculate carpets from wall to nearly every wall, and a huge, spotless basement as dry as the Sahara. But the house seemed to have been designed for a sunny, poolside, blizzard-free life in some sweaty suburb in southern California; throughout the entire winter, ice sealed shut the sliding doors from the living room to the back porch. Worse, far worse, we were a half-hour drive over a wretched highway from every pleasure, convenience, and obligation in Halifax. What could possibly have inspired me to buy such a place? Well, it was just a short walk from Prospect Bay and the mooring I would install for the sailboat I just had to own. Such is the power of yachting dreams.

On our street, which was short, bare, treeless, and unpaved, a dozen or so assistant professors, sales directors, and middle managers lived with their wives and children in more of these nondescript bungalows of the times. Like us, they were all come-from-aways, and quite soon the neighbourhood felt like neither us nor Nova Scotia. The schools were crappy, the shopping skimpy, the backyards rocky, the neighbours both gloomy and gossipy, and, more often than not, the doctor tipsy. A cloud of disappointment seemed to enshroud everything, but maybe it was just my own.

The drive to Halifax was only sixteen miles long, but always took at least half an hour to complete because the road was only two lanes wide and, in my memory anyway, its traffic mostly consisted of rusty autos spewing clouds of black exhaust and wavering pickups loaded with old sofas, fridges, and mattresses. This was the kind of road where you pass the occasional little house that needs both a paint job and someone who cares enough not to leave Christmas decorations hanging off it all year long. Having reached Halifax, I parked on the fifth level of the lot at Scotia Square and, while walking to an elevator up to the head office of Nova Scotia Light and Power, always got a little kick of pleasure just from catching an open-air glimpse of the harbour.

My chief responsibility was to edit *Utilect*, a quarterly magazine for the company's 1,100 or so employees. It published news about promotions, retirements, awards, dances, picnics, hobbies, and company teams, etc. But it also carried stories I wrote about the shipwrecks that led to Sable Island's reputation as "The Graveyard of the Atlantic," the punishment that "The Year Without A Summer," 1816, inflicted on Nova Scotians, and other intriguing chunks of Bluenose history.

What had happened to me anyway? Successful journalists in Toronto saw themselves as the cream of the profession in Canada, and my friends there found it totally incomprehensible that I'd retreated to such a distant dead-end as Halifax and gone to work as the editor of a corporate house organ. Did Gordy Howe quit the Detroit Red Wings to satisfy a burning desire to score goals for the St. Petersburg Suns? Did Bobby Orr abandon the Boston Bruins to help the Des Moines Oak Leaves win the Turner Cup? Okay, I hadn't been an Orr or Howe of our trade but, as a competent journeyman, had played in their league and seen a fair bit of ice time.

I told no one in Toronto but, truth was, I did feel a trifle out of place at NSLPC, and not entirely welcome. Leon Major, Toronto-born like me, knew the feeling. A celebrated opera director at age thirty, he moved to Halifax in 1963 to become the Neptune Theatre's first artistic director, and never forgot that, during a South End cocktail party to "welcome" him, a pugnacious burgher demanded, "If you're so good, Major, why are you here?" Working for Light and Power in a dozen windowless cubicles, I sensed that the more seasoned employees in nearby cubbyholes like mine nursed similar questions about me. Each undoubtedly knew a true, blue Nova Scotian who was vastly better qualified to edit *Utilect* than some know-it-all dork parachuted in from Upper Canada.

When I griped in *Utilect* – humourously, I thought – about an April blizzard that blasted Nova Scotia while thousands of golfers and June sunshine were busting out all over my dear old southern Ontario homeland, two floormates of mine, junior managers of some sort in their early thirties, kept glaring at me as though struggling to suppress that eternal reply to the fault-finding newcomer: "If you don't like it here, why don't you just get the hell back to where you came from?"

If they didn't get my little joke about local weather, what they did find funny, screamingly funny, was my confession that, while I drove to Kentville one morning, the damn fog, the Nova Scotia fog, was so thick over Highway 102 that I passed Shubenacadie before realizing I'd missed the 101 turnoff to Kentville way back at Sackville. Hah! So the hotshot from Hog Town got lost in the fog on the busiest highway in the province. That was so stupid it somehow made these two bozos decide that maybe I was tolerable after all.

The top dog on our floor was the tidy and terse boss of the Marketing Division and Customer Service. He was a Mason, an elder in a Presbyterian church, a brigadier-general in the Canadian Forces Reserve, and, in short, not someone likely to get along swimmingly with a hard-drinking, free-thinking, imported journalist who'd dropped out of both the United Church of Canada and the Canadian University Naval Training Division. Nor did it endear me to him that if I had good reason to dislike any order he gave me, I could appeal it directly to the president of the company, the infinitely wiser A.R. Harrington.

Relations between me and the brigadier-general were testy at best but, for quite a while there, I was the most insignificant of irritants, a gnat, compared to an elephantine crisis in customer relations. The company had so disastrously bungled the turning over of its billing system to its first mainframe computer that tens of thousands of customers were getting wildly inaccurate electricity bills. Some bills were ludicrously low, others horrifyingly high. To solve this mess, Nova Scotia Light and Power stole a computer expert from its biggest competitor and worst enemy, the government-owned Nova Scotia Power Commission. To get him to cross the line, it gave him a vice-presidency, thus putting severely out of joint the noses of long-time executives who thought they deserved the appointment more.

The computer apparatus at the heart of the problem was inside a metal box as big as a railroad freight car. That sat in a room with temperature, humidity, and ventilation controls comparable to those in the intensive care unit of a hospital. The No Smoking rule on the door was black and big enough to suggest that anyone who broke it would be fired on the spot. Since the new vice-president's staff, including the operators here, were battling one of the most complicated challenges in Light and Power's history, I chose them as my cover story for one edition of *Utilect*. I wrote the piece myself, called it "The Computer People," and accompanied it with plenty of photos of them at work.

A pretty good effort, I thought, but other departments complained about my having celebrated the computer team while completely ignoring them and the vitally important work they did. What about the sales people, the engineering people, or the linemen people, for heaven's sake? Since personal computers had yet to be invented, and the glory days of YouTube, Facebook, and Twitter were half a human lifetime away, I learned about this disgruntlement primarily from face-to-face encounters. It dawned on me then that no one had ever managed to edit any magazine – for nurses, welders, florists, architects, rug hookers, orchid growers, ukulele players, or whomever – without pissing off someone somewhere.

Late in July, I wrote a story for another magazine that pissed off no less a Nova Scotian than the premier of the province, and thereby elevated myself from gnat-sized irritant at Light and Power to spectacular saboteur. If I owed my first lesson in the intimacy of Bluenose politics to Robert Stanfield back in 1963, it was from a Liberal premier, the cockier and more impulsive Gerald A. Regan, that I now got my second.

It was much less pleasant. Advance warning came one hot afternoon when a friend I bumped into at a downtown liquor store told me, "Boy, is Gabby ever mad at you! He's just white with rage!" What was this guy talking about? Who was Gabby? That, it turned out, was Regan. Since working as a young sports announcer on radio, Gabby had been his nickname.

The next morning, the president of Light and Power, and my boss there, Harrington, told me *Saturday Night* magazine in Toronto had just published a story of mine that not only mocked Regan but so enraged him he demanded I be fired. Harrington demurred, but then Regan called J.C. MacKeen, the chairman of NSLPC and supreme poobah among business bigshots of Halifax, to tell him to tell Harrington to fire me. Not four months had passed since, emboldened by the promise of a feeble but reliable income from Light and Power, I'd exiled myself and family from the jobs, markets, comfort, and familiarity of our home and native province to settle as "come-from-aways" on a cold, alien, and merciless coast.

Again, however, Harrington bravely refused to bounce me. He merely told me the premier's demand was strike one against me, the chairman's strike two, and he himself was just about ready to throw strike-three-and-yer-out. Never, for as long as I worked at his company, was I ever to submit to any publication any writing about any aspect of Nova Scotia politics without first getting him to approve every word of it. Already then, I had cleverly arranged for myself a journalistic career in which my boss was my eagle-eyed censor.

What had I written to make Regan so apoplectic? I had arrived in Nova Scotia just as he was pushing himself to the head of a pack of politicians baying for the revival of an ancient ambition: to "harness" the stupendous tides of the Bay of Fundy and thus generate miraculous supplies of electric energy. According to this pie-in-the-sky prospect, Fundy Tidal Power (FTP) would produce eternal flows of pollution-free and inflation-proof electricity not only for domestic use but for limitless and "insatiable" U.S. markets. Thus, Regan predicted, "Vast profits were inevitable." Not only that, FTP would inspire the foundation of dozens of new industries, create 20,000 jobs, and, for visitors who find big dams irresistible, blossom as a gigantic tourist mecca. All in all, it could not help but "dramatically alter the economy of our province."

He had therefore established the Nova Scotia Tidal Power Corporation; given it a budget of $10 million ($67 million in 2020 dollars); appointed as its head the notoriously abrasive Bluenose industrialist R.B. ("Bobby") Cameron; and revealed that his government's FTP negotiations with private concerns had reached "the deadly serious stage." Interests of stupendous clout seemed to be involved. Consolidated Edison in New York. The banking group of Baron Edmund de Rothschild in Europe. Rothschild, Regan allowed, was organizing a tidal power consortium of some forty companies, and what could sound more effective and omnipotent than a big, fat, juicy, and slightly mysterious "consortium"?

Not only at home but in Boston, New York, and France, Regan immersed himself in his self-invented role as the Father of FTP. In New York, he revealed Nova Scotia's intention "to harness the Bay of Fundy so Con Ed won't have brown-outs here anymore," and his "target date for major development of tide energy to come on stream" was 1980. But it was in France that his flair for publicity blossomed like a giant sunflower. For it was there that he led the biggest government-sponsored, overseas junket in the history of Nova Scotia on what the Halifax *Chronicle Herald* obligingly called "his personal tour of the world's major successful tidal power project."

This was (and still is) on the estuary of the Rance River in Brittany, and its "success" was questionable. It produced nowhere near even 1 percent of the electricity generated in France and did so at a cost so high French authorities refused to discuss it. Associated Press therefore dismissed the plant as "a fine tourist attraction and a dandy bridge." Yet Regan had in tow not only his press secretary but the managing editor of *The Chronicle Herald*, the boss of his new tidal power outfit, the boss of the provincially owned Nova Scotia Power Commission, two cabinet ministers, three executives of the crown corporation Industrial Estates Limited, and assorted wives. The whole adventure, he said with becoming modesty, "constitutes the most successful undertaking of this nature that the province has ever been involved in."

Newcomer though I was, I could not believe any politician in the history of the Maritimes had ever proved so expensively inventive at exploiting a project for publicity favourable to himself than Regan had with the FTP pipe dream. And pipe dream it was. Seasoned engineers at Light and Power told me stupendous technical and financial problems stood in the way of converting the world's highest and strongest tides into usable electricity, and predicted no one would solve these until well into the twenty-first century. I could not help thinking that, with respect to this latest FTP hoopla, led by Regan, someone should stand up and shout the slogan that writers Jimmy Breslin and Norman Mailer used while campaigning for election to the New York City Council: "No More Bullshit."

I just couldn't resist. I had spent seventeen years among journalists in Ottawa and especially Toronto who saw skepticism as indispensable to their work; the exposure of corruption by politicians as their supreme achievement; general shit-disturbing as a professional duty; and the publication of informed, pointed, rude, and raucous argy-bargy about mighty government projects as a common good.

It was only natural then for me to write a four thousand-word story that, boiled to its essence, said this: "The horny hands and steel-cable forearms of the best dairy farmer in all of Nova Scotia has never, ever, managed to milk a cow dryer than the Honourable Gerald A. Regan has milked the idea of Fundy Tidal Power." The venerable *Saturday Night* magazine, read mostly by Canadians whom populists might now denounce as "the elite," published the entire story and entitled it "The Great Fundy Hot Air Project."

For the next four months I quietly did my *Utilect* duty, refrained from writing anything even remotely connected to Nova Scotia politics for any publication whatsoever, and gradually absorbed bits of background about the less than amiable relationship between Light and Power and the Nova Scotia Power Commission. Light and Power was one of the last big privately owned electric utilities in Canada. The Power Commission was a crown corporation owned by the provincial government. Light and Power dominated the lucrative electricity markets in both Halifax and the province's second-biggest city, Sydney. In 1970, it racked up profits of $4 million ($27 million in 2020 currency). The Power Commission's customers, spread out in towns and rural settlements, were harder and more expensive to serve. In 1970, it lost $371,000 (the equivalent of $2.5 million in 2020). Harrington and Les Kirkpatrick, president of the commission, were equally aggressive and equally contemptuous of each other.

Light and Power was not only in fine shape financially but also considerably bigger than its government-owned rival. Still, most provinces now owned the utilities that generated and distributed almost all the electricity sold within their borders, and the distinct and horrible possibility of a government takeover had hung over Light and Power for as long as anyone could remember. And that's how things stood on December 3, 1971.

All that afternoon, with a reporter from *The Globe and Mail*, I drank draught beer at the Seahorse Tavern on Argyle Street. (Public relations men in those days were supposed to drink beer with newspapermen, and anyway it was Friday.) The Seahorse, incidentally, was below sidewalk level and only twenty-three years old but, having opened in 1948 as Halifax's first legal tavern since 1921, it was as historically important to us tipplers as Province House was to political scientists.

At 5:30, I dropped in on Light and Power to pick up a file of research I'd left on my desk. I assumed it was now safe to exhale my Seahorse-ripened breath up there because any senior executives who happened to be frowners upon beer-swillers would already have gone for the weekend. But when an elevator discharged me at my floor, I saw to my horror that the joint was crawling with just about the whole gang of Light and Power big cheeses.

Vice-presidents, division heads, marketing chiefs, top engineers, they all stood around in awkward postures as though stunned, uncertain where to step next, or perhaps even holding back tears. With speed that had knocked them off balance, the old and dreaded nightmare had come true. No sooner had stock markets closed for the weekend than Regan had announced his government's launching of a hostile stock market bid to take over Light and Power, and thereby guarantee the despised Power Commission would gobble it up.

Could these executives already hear the flushing of their careers down a commission toilet? A couple, I thought, looked at me as though I smelled a lot worse than Oland beer. Had it crossed their minds that, until I'd showed up only eight months before, their company had escaped the evil clutches of government since before the Dirty Thirties? I ducked out of there fast.

Light and Power, whose directors included arch-capitalist luminaries of the Bluenose business community, loudly denounced the takeover not only because they agreed with the Halifax *Chronicle Herald* that it was "a high-handed assault on the free-enterprise system" but, more important, because they wanted more per share than the $13 the government had offered. They didn't get it. The offer was already $5 higher than the December 3 price on the Toronto Stock Exchange, and by January 27, 1972, the government had 90 percent of the shares. Game over. The government's Power Commission emerged as its new Nova Scotia Power Corporation, and Light and Power vanished inside that.

Not seven years later, however, Regan may have regretted his stock market coup. In the election of 1978, the anger Nova Scotians felt about increases in the electricity bills they got from his government's utility helped the Conservatives, led by John Buchanan, to thrash him and his Liberals. Then in 1992, twenty years after Regan provincialized Light and Power, the government of Premier Donald Cameron faced such heavy pressure to control a skyrocketing deficit that it privatized its entire province-wide electric utility. The free enterprise system had rebounded from that high-handed assault. For two decades now, Nova Scotia Power, along with half a dozen utilities in the U.S. and Caribbean, has been a wholly owned subsidiary of the Halifax-based Emera Inc.

And tidal power? In the early 1980s, Nova Scotia Power did build the Annapolis Royal Generating Station, which still converts the Fundy tides that roll up the Annapolis River into enough electricity to power four thousand homes. It's the only tidal power station in North America, but compared to the gorgeous feast of benefits that, half a century ago, Regan promised FTP would deliver, remains little more than a burp. The urgent need for energy generation that's both sustainable and makes no contribution to climate change has recently combined with advances in technology to inspire governments and companies here and in Europe to experiment with the sinking on Fundy seabeds of turbines as high as five storeys. Alas, the world's most muscular tides crippled and mutilated underwater installations, and financial crises have driven away investors. No one can yet say just when the tides of Fundy will power the air conditioners of Manhattan, the electric toothbrushes of Connecticut, or the unborn industries of New Brunswick and Nova Scotia.

But back to early '72: the Power Commission's swallowing of Light and Power cost Harrington his job, but not me mine. I was now a kind of civil servant in limbo, and Gabby was my ultimate boss. I waited for his axe to fall. That would have freed me to brag that the Honourable Gerald A. Regan had spent tens of millions of taxpayers' dollars just to bounce me, but I was already too harmless to be noticed and had to quit to get out of there. I landed a job as host of CBC television's beloved suppertime talk show, *Gazette*, and quickly proved to be the worst in its history.

5

My Short, Grisly Career as a TV Superstar

Whenever I see youngsters today addressing crowds from a stage, their easy and frequently eloquent flow of words surprises me. Where did they get such confidence? At thirteen, I was a quivering, choking, sweating, tongue-tied, and terrified victim of glossophobia. That's the fear of public speaking, and apparently it's more widespread even than the fear of death, snakes, spiders, or heights. Some experts say it stems from a fear of rejection that goes all the way back to prehistoric times when being expelled from your group meant being torn apart by a predator. Well, maybe. All I know is that, compared to standing behind a podium to address even the most sympathetic audience, snakes and spiders are no more frightening than ladybugs.

Stumbling to my feet to answer teachers' questions in grade ten, I was frail, skinny, faltering, and spoke in a barely audible mutter. "Speak up, speak up,

Bruce," one teacher finally bellowed. "For God's sake, SPEAK UP!" He sounded as though I was not merely annoying but such a contemptible wimp that, 70,000 years ago, he'd have expelled me from the tribe to face sabretooth tigers by myself.

Every bout of glossophobia made apprehension about the next one worse than ever. The night before delivering my only lecture during three years at Mount A, I tried to squelch my rumbling volcano of fear by downing much rum with a couple of friends. I thus added a sickening hangover to the glossophobia that afflicted me the next morning while I struggled to enlighten a dozen or so English Lit students about hidden meanings in *Ulysses* by James Joyce.

My audience mostly came from farms and small towns in the Maritimes. This was not a notably sophisticated part of the world, and the odds were high that the few Maritimers who had actually read *Ulysses* still agreed with the "smut-hounds" who had damned it decades before as filthy, obscene, blasphemous, corrupting, and just rotten to its core. It would certainly not have been on the favourite reading lists of United Church clergymen. One of these was the president of Mount A, and scores of others who had earned their degrees here. Among the listeners to my insights into *Ulysses* on that painful morning so long ago were daughters of clergymen and teetotalling youths destined for ordainment.

With head pounding, body shaky, and mouth as dry as sandpaper, I tried to compensate for my condition by enunciating with extra clarity. I was practically shouting when I explained that Joyce, while writing *Ulysses*, had sought to depict the city of Dublin not as a living organism, but as "A GIGANTIC, LIVING ORGASM!"

Stunned silence greeted this rare piece of literary analysis. No one laughed, giggled, or even looked at me.

Gazing out a window, I said, "Um, I mean 'organism.' Heh, Heh. I guess this novel affected me more than I thought."

The professor who'd assigned me the lecture, a young Torontonian, exploded in laughter so wild I thought he'd fall from his chair.

During the sixty-five years since that morning I have never quite overcome my dread of speechifying. In May 2013, as my seventy-ninth birthday approached, I was obliged to address 350 journalists at an awards banquet and, knowing I'd never manage to do it ad-lib, wrote in advance every word of a speech I would simply read aloud. I kept this down to three minutes but was so apprehensive it took me four full days to compose.

For every journalist I've ever known, talking on radio was as easy as relaxing over a beer, but I could never do it without my voice trembling and wavering. For me, competently interviewing anyone on television was unimaginable, and that's why I jumped at the chance to play host on CBC Halifax's TV talk show, *Gazette*. Since it was ridiculous and humiliating for a mature journalist like myself to be terrified of performing on television, I would conquer my fear forever by defying it five suppertimes per week. And just to bolster my resolve, the job paid $18,200 per year, a fat-cat income by Nova Scotian standards in 1982 (and equivalent to $114,000 in today's currency).

I beat out competitors for the job by choosing to interview for my audition a charming and garrulous storyteller named Jack Brayley. He was chief of the Halifax bureau of Canadian Press, a friend and long-time underling of my father at CP, and a raconteur about Bluenose news that had been breaking for decades. I couldn't miss.

Jack was so entertaining that the judges of the audition mistakenly decided I was an ace interviewer. As one CBC executive put it, "Bruce is the man for *Gazette*. He's not too ugly, he's not too handsome. He's not too stupid, he's not too smart. Bruce is the sort of fellow you'd like to drink a couple of beers with out back when you should be mowing your grass."

That particular broadcasting authority had no idea that never again would I conduct an interview as good as the one with Jack, which the public would not see. Nor did it occur to him that some of *Gazette*'s most loyal viewers might take an instant dislike to me not only as a boorish interloper at a family party but, more justly, as a blundering amateur contaminating the performance of beloved and smooth-talking pros.

Eighteen years old, *Gazette* was the longest-running suppertime talk show on Canadian television, and two of its original personalities were not only still with it but, like fine wine, improving with each passing year. They were Don Tremaine, announcer, master of light conversation, and the most recognized broadcaster in the Maritimes, and Rube Hornstein, intrepid interviewer and a weatherman whose TV experience was unmatched anywhere in the country. Rube, Don, and *Gazette* were Nova Scotia institutions, like the schooner *Bluenose* and equalization payments, and one did not take lightly one's on-camera adventures with the likes of them.

There was too much heritage to honour, too many boots to fill. *Gazette*'s first host had been Max Ferguson, whose inimitable wit on CBC radio and television would delight millions of Canadians for half a century. Then came Lloyd MacInnis, a performer of legendary on-camera suavity. My immediate predecessor in the job was a comely and intelligent young woman for whom chatting on television, and getting others chatting on television, seemed as natural as breathing. She had the double advantage of bearing a quintessential Nova Scotian name, Marilyn MacDonald, and having been born in Cape Breton. (As an objective come-from-away, I've noticed that Cape Breton Islanders' loyalty to Cape Breton Islanders is even more powerful than the loyalty to one another of Nova Scotians as a whole.)

When I joined the show, Marilyn was pregnant and would not be back. Don and Rube were both on temporary leave, and *Gazette*, for its most faithful viewers, did not seem to be there anymore. What had CBC done with it? Where were the regulars? The best faces were the old faces. Bring them back. "Where does that Harry Bruce come from?" one of my earliest non-fans called the CBC to ask. "He has such a flat accent." With deadly accuracy, the switchboard replied, "As far as I know, he's from Toronto." Not the ideal hometown for the host of *Gazette*.

I had been here little more than a year, the tiniest fraction of the time it normally took a come-from-away to graduate into the ranks of true-blue Nova

Scotians. Mellish "Ironman" Lane, probably the best baseball pitcher in Nova Scotia history and one of the first inductees into the province's Sports Hall of Fame, was born in Lunenburg but once told me the town had never accepted him as a true Lunenburger. And why not? His father had been born in Prince Edward Island, that's why. Fathers counted for a lot in Nova Scotians' assessments of newcomers, job applicants, potential business partners, etc.

I soon found it convenient to answer questions about my birthplace by saying, "Well, yes, I'm from Toronto, but my father was from Guysborough County." This seemed to slightly thaw my interrogators. Hmmph. Well, maybe that's something in his favour.

Trouble was, I couldn't very well tell *Gazette* viewers five suppertimes per week that although I was born in Hog Town my father was from these very sea-bound coasts, and the daily reports on phone calls from viewers continued to reveal distressing concerns about my possible origin. "What is the name of the new host on *Gazette*?" Answer: Harry Bruce. "Well, send him back to whatever rock he crawled out from." The switchboard kindly listed that little exchange as an Inquiry rather than a Bad Comment, but in most cases it had little choice: "This program has turned into something terrible. That Bruce is not capable, and did not need to be imported ... Who is that shaggy-haired man on *Gazette* now doing an interview? He looks like something that came out of Toronto."

My hairstyle truly was a hangover from life in Toronto. Big, thick, bushy, and frizzy, it was still what a friend up there had dubbed an "Afro-Wasp" cut. It inspired one *Gazette* viewer to complain, "That little old lady sitting between Rube and Don needs to go to the barber and try to get himself looking like a man."

From my first moments on *Gazette*, viewers mercilessly listed faults I'd never known were mine: "That new host is slovenly, sloppy, and slouching, not fit to be on the program ... Now that Don is back, why have we got that Bruce still on? ... We are sick of him spoiling the program and [unkindest cut of all] he can't even use the Queen's English correctly. I am taking up a petition to have him removed."

Alas for such sourpusses, that would not be easy. My contract guaranteed I could stammer in my hairy, amateurish fashion before tens of thousands of Maritimers five nights a week for a whole year, including Christmas Day.

Probably the lowest point among all the low points in this career was the icy morning I stood under a sign at the Atlantic Winter Fair that declared "East Is East, West Is West. PEI Potatoes Are The Best." Clutching a microphone in one hand and a pamphlet entitled Potatoes With Love in the other, I flopped around in a limp conversation with two young P.E.I. potato promoters about the trillions of tons of spuds that leave the island each year and, well, you'd be surprised, you really would, by all the marvelous things you could do with them.

Rotten little kids kept heckling and bumping me, the producer wrung his hands, the sound man fiddled and scowled, the cameraman smirked in the superior way of cameramen, and the lighting man beamed the evil tools of his trade so that they not only blinded me but made the sweat pop from my face. And there I was, talking about "potato power" and fighting the shakes, and my voice was wavering, and I was thinking, "What have I done to a once promising career in journalism?" My misery combined with my lack of potato commitment in such a depressing way that the CBC killed the interview, but I thought it was no worse than dozens of others I'd done that had aired. If I'd been a viewer who'd tuned into my discussions with Halifax's only real live North Vietnamese – or the boss who bribed his employees to quit smoking, the world's foremost woman authority on man-eating sharks, the cigar-smoking chick from California who'd made a film about an art school for feminists, or the leader of something called the Linguistic Orchestra and Prose Quintet – I'd have quickly switched to whatever soap opera I could find that late in the day.

No teenaged journalism student could have failed to make gripping the report of a Halifax sports fan who had been at the Munich Olympics when Palestinian terrorists massacred eleven Israeli athletes, but somehow I did. Nor did I perform better with survivors of a South African jail, a factory in China, injustice in Uganda, various horrors in Pakistan, rotten food in Moscow, political crises in West Germany, traffic jams in Ottawa, or cultural indignities along the Digby shore.

I rapped feebly with lifeguards, lumberjacks, pacifists, biologists, nutritionists, ecologists, test pilots, Chinese cooks, soldiers, sailors, doctors, lawyers, do-gooders, stuffed shirts, and, forever, politicians. With experts, I was an equalizer. I made them equally boring. Experts on day care, dental care, care of the aged, care of cats and dogs, and the winter care of your camper trailer. Experts on the oil industry, hate literature, obscene phone calls, the rights of the unborn, and the rights of those who wanted to abort the unborn. I interviewed one expert on how to be a gourmet and a nationalist at the same time, another on how to apply behavioural psychology to the coaching of basketball teams, and still another on what to do when you find maimed people on a highway. Everyone was always an expert on something. Except me.

I gradually came to realize that, just as my audition with Jack Brayley had indicated, the quality of the interview had little to do with the quality of the interviewer. Everything depended on the guest. If he or she were good, I scarcely needed to be there and, indeed, there were respects in which I was not. The moment a guest began to roll along, gesticulating, shouting, and caring, the cameras cut me out entirely.

Farley Mowat, the celebrity author, celebrity environmentalist, and celebrity egocentric, talked loudly and lustily about the horrors we humans were inflicting on Nature, and punctuated his rich flow of holier-than-thou-and-thou invective by turning to me regularly and saying, "Harry." He so thrilled *Gazette*'s producers that, for the first and only time, they sent me frantic signals to let a guest keep right on yammering for twice as long as scheduled. As Mowat left the studio, CBC veterans told me, "Great interview, Harry, great interview." I blushed prettily. During twenty minutes, I had asked Mowat perhaps five questions, two of which were, "Would you care to expand on that point, Farley?"

If Mowat had no particular need for me, neither did Pierre Berton. He was another superb writer of non-fiction, and also another big-feeling veteran of talking on television. Neither ever let an ounce of modesty weaken the volume of his opinionating. My interview with Berton was excellent, thank you very much, but my ten-year-old daughter could have done it as well. No matter what I asked ex-broadcaster René Lévesque, the galvanic leader of Québec separatism, he was fascinating and loquacious and, in their own way, so were three bright and beautiful young strippers from a downtown Halifax club called Cousin Brucie's (no relation).

Actors, singers, strippers, and anyone else who made a living by holding the attention of crowds could seldom resist turning themselves on for *Gazette*'s cameras, if not for me. I felt I had little more to do with what was unfolding than the nearby potted plant. Having donned a sky-blue shirt, silk tie, and pricey business suit, having had a cosmetician dab stuff on my face, and a coiffeur unhappily mess with my hair and ask me once again why I didn't use a conditioner, I would sit among pushy cameras and glaring lights, and try to look interested in the chattering on of someone I had never seen before. I was a living prop. I had little influence, and no control.

As a writer, I had total control. I alone. My tools were blank paper, ballpoint pens, and a typewriter. I needed no astronomically expensive collection of cameras, tripods, speakers, monitors, microphones, and harsh, blazing lights, no control rooms, and no squads of engineers and technicians of this and that. My office was at home, and sometimes as big as our living room, other times as tiny as a clothes closet. With a steno pad and ballpoint, I could write in a café or a hotel room, on a beach or the back seat of a car. I was free, and what I created, good or bad, was all mine.

Five months at *Gazette* diluted my dread of appearing on television. The job terrified me no longer. It merely filled me with an unhealthy mixture of apprehension and boredom. Lights, cameras, action! And ho-hum. Thus, I was neither shocked nor appalled when the senior producer of *Gazette* invited me into his office and confided that he was not entirely pleased with my "development as a television personality."

Go on, I said. Really? Gosh, that sounds like a vote of no confidence. I guess I'd better exercise the thirty-day escape clause in our contract, hadn't I? Back to pen and ink, and the satisfying clatter of my late father's old manual Underwood.

For a few miraculous minutes late one night in 1977 I actually enjoyed appearing on a TV talk show. This time, I was not the host, but an uncharacteristically relaxed guest. The host was Peter Gzowski, and the show was *90 Minutes Live*. While starring on CBC radio's *This Country in the Morning* for three years, he had proven a phenomenally good interviewer. Deciding he should do for late-night television viewers what he'd done for mid-morning radio listeners, CBC had invented *90 Minutes Live* and plunked him down as its host.

I was a guest on a night it was broadcast from Halifax, from the old CBC-TV building on Bell Road. Seated beside me was my fellow guest, the witty and multitalented, multimedia writer Silver Don Cameron. Peter, Don, Harry. Media guys. We knew one another. Let the stories flow.

Don lived in the Acadian village of D'Escousse on Isle Madame in Richmond County, Cape Breton Island, and the story that flowed from him was about a legendary performance decades before in the provincial legislature. It starred one Isadore LeBlanc, the Honourable Member for Richmond. Declaiming with his heavy Acadian accent, LeBlanc made such a nuisance of himself with his incessant demands for the construction of a bridge to Isle Madame that the premier finally rose to declare, once and for all, that such a bridge was out of the question. It would have to cross Lennox Passage, and that was such a large body of water the bridge would be prohibitively expensive. The government would never build it.

LeBlanc shouted, "De Premier says de bridge would be too h'expensive because Lennox Passage is a big body of water. But h'it's not big. Hell, I could piss halfways across!"

"Shame! Shame!" cried Honourable Members. "Order! Order! You're out of order."

And the voice of LeBlanc boomed above all others, "You're damned right I'm h'out of h'order. H'if I was in order I could piss all de ways across."

Isle Madame got its bridge in 1919.

The story that best flowed from me on *90 Minutes Live* described a shameful stunt I pulled during my dismal career on *Gazette* in 1972. Since I had had nothing to do on camera during the pre-taped interviews that ate up big chunks of *Gazette*, I often waited until a pretaped segment began, and then sneaked right out of the CBC building. I walked briskly up Bell Road for the length of a couple of football fields, and ducked into Sullivan's bar, which was just below street level in the ten-storey office building at the Willow Tree intersection.

As I sat down directly in front of the TV, Ralph, the bartender, said, "Good evening, Mr. Bruce. The usual?"

That was a double amber rum with a splash of water over two ice cubes. Since I invariably appeared on one of the pre-taped interviews, Ralph's next question was, "And would you like to watch yourself on *Gazette*, Mr. Bruce?"

So there I smugly sat, watching my show unfold for a few delicious minutes. At the right time, I walked back to the CBC building and through a rear door to rejoin the *Gazette* gang, with nobody the wiser. But late one suppertime after I'd downed only half my drink, disaster struck. A tangled mess of flashing lines and blinking patterns completely obliterated the interview I was watching and seconds later, Don Tremaine filled the screen. With his deep, confident voice, he assured viewers, "We're having some technical problems just now, ladies and gentlemen, but the host of our show, Harry Bruce, will be right with us to help us carry on."

I sprinted out of the bar and down Bell Road so fast that by the time I ripped open the back door of the CBC building, calls of "Harry Bruce ... Haaarry Bruce" still echoed in the corridors. I ducked into a Men's room, caught my breath, and prepared my lies: "Well, you see, this morning I seemed to have caught a touch of the flu that's been going around Halifax, but I came to work anyway, and then a few minutes ago it gave me this terrible attack of diarrhea, and I had to find a Men's room fast. Technical problems? You needed me in the studio? Geez, I'm so sorry."

I learned later that if there were such a thing as capital punishment at the CBC, it would be reserved for any TV host found guilty of actually vanishing while his show was airing.

No one at the CBC doubted my story until, five years later, my old buddy Peter came to town with *90 Minutes Live*. He was not a happy man. If I had flopped on regional TV, he was now flopping on national TV. He'd been a sensational hit as a radio interviewer, but was now a stumblebum as a television interviewer. At least, that was the consensus among critics, and *90 Minutes Live* lasted only two years. I happened to think he was pretty good, by comparison with me anyway. I met him for lunch a few hours before appearing on his show and, as an old hand at screwing up on TV, told him all about my fictional attack of flu. Strictly between him and me, of course.

But no sooner had the laughter subsided after Don's story about Isadore LeBlanc than Peter blindsided me. Was a certain story he'd heard about my having repeatedly played hooky from *Gazette* really true? Would I please tell Canada (including my children) all about that? So out it came. Sullivan's, Ralph, the rum, the crazy, jiggling mess on the screen, the dash down Bell Road, the dose of the runs I invented. Possibly because my confession showed that a TV host could do something even worse than a lousy interview, it seemed to delight Peter. Remembering that night, I'm sure that Don and I together gave him a few of the most entertaining minutes in the short, ignominious life of his *90 Minutes Live*.

6

Our Oldest Neighbour, the Ocean

In the excitement of quitting Toronto for Halifax, I overlooked what I was abandoning. Toronto had begun to shed everything that, in my schooldays, had given it a reputation as churchy, straitlaced, joyless, greedy, narrow-minded, bigoted, and boring. It had also been the most British city outside Britain. In grade-school classes, teachers led us in spirited renditions of "The British Grenadiers." In high school, we learned that Canada's greatest heroes were British major-generals, James Wolfe at the Battle of the Plains of Abraham, and Isaac Brock at the Battle of Queenston Heights. The Toronto I grew up in treasured all things bright and British, from Big Ben, Oxford U, the Royal Navy, and Rolls-Royce sedans to Burberry trench coats, Dundee marmalades, Sheffield knives, and roast beef with Yorkshire pudding. Canada's flag still had the Union Jack in one corner.

By the late '60s, Canada had its own flag, and Toronto's spectacular, new "clamshell" city hall had opened. Designed by Finns (not Brits), winners of a contest that architects from forty-two nations entered, it declared this was a city that deserved the world's attention. Toronto certainly got attention from immigrants. The floodtide had begun. They poured in from all over Western Europe and South Asia, and from Russia, China, Cambodia, Vietnam, and the Caribbean. Between 1951, when I turned seventeen, and 1971, the population of Metropolitan Toronto more than doubled to 2.6 million. It was now Canada's financial capital, hottest theatre town, and biggest and most multicultural city. It would soon boast more than 160 spoken languages, thousands of restaurants, glorious festivals, a sizzling nightlife, and repeated rankings as the most livable city in the world.

And I had left this blossoming urban miracle for Halifax? How smart was that? Now that this was not just a place where I'd frittered away one summer as a naval cadet and occasionally visited as a reporter, but the new hometown in which I'd settled with my family for countless years to come, I began to wonder if it didn't lack a certain cosmopolitan spirit. Though an international port with five universities, it felt less like a vibrant, welcoming, open-minded, and sophisticated city than a stodgy provincial town. A big Truro.

It was only slowly emerging from times when Catholics and Protestants jealously guarded their separate domains in education and separate rights in politics; when Catholics and Jews were barred from chartered accountancy, and Blacks and Jews from the Halifax and Waegwoltic clubs; when professors viciously ridiculed young women to discourage them from continuing at medical or law school. At lunchtime, hordes of men downed draft beer and cheap steaks at joints like the Derby Tavern on Gottingen Street, but never in the company of women. They were still barred from taverns.

The legalization of the public consumption of beer, wine, and spirits was occurring so slowly and prissily you'd have thought the government was run by a bunch of Sunday school teachers. Even after women gained entry to taverns, it remained illegal for men and women to drink in public together. At the Midtown, the city's most famous and beloved tavern, the arrival of women drinkers was such a novelty that their washroom was all too obviously a management afterthought. To reach it, they had to navigate their way through the kitchen, past the meat locker, and up a flight of stairs.

The province allowed you to have two glasses of draft beer sitting in front of you on a table in a tavern but no more. If a friend arrived to join your party, you could not carry your two glasses to a bigger table. You had to get a waiter to do that. If you were just one of the boys, however, you could at least feel welcome, and reasonably safe. Homosexual couples were refused service in many bars and, if they walked outdoors at night downtown, risked bloody or even fatal beatings.

Comic actress Cathy Jones remembered visiting Halifax in the early '80s, and calling it "City of the Living Dead … We thought of it as horrible; dull, racist, boring, redneck." And she's a Newfoundlander!

I wouldn't have attacked Halifax quite as fiercely as she did, but it did strike me as more inclined to give a thumbs-down than to offer high-fives. As that shaggy-haired man on *Gazette*, I had first-hand knowledge of at least some Haligonians' distrust of newcomers. But in addition to suspicion, a stifling sameness characterized much of Halifax life. The city's only diversity seemed to lie in its crazy weather. Most of Halifax's 260,000 people (one-tenth of Toronto's) were descendants of long-gone settlers from the British Isles. Overwhelmingly dominant, these were seemingly content that, among more than two hundred local restaurants, few served anything other than the blandest Canadian "home cooking" or greasiest Chinese-Canadian chow. If there'd been a vote to name the best restaurant in town, the hands-down winner would have been a spot near the Dockyard called Camille's Fish & Chips.

Two brave exceptions to my sour generalizations about Halifax eateries were noted in 1976 by none other than the most celebrated restaurant critic in the U.S., Craig Claiborne of *The New York Times*. He was delighted to find that Halifax in late March was not the icebound Arctic outpost he'd expected but "a place of quiet charms, moderate temperature and two restaurants that, if you happen to be in Nova Scotia, may well be worth a detour."

The first of these was The Five Fishermen, which opened in 1975 in a building on Argyle Street opposite the Grand Parade, and still serves its superior seafood there. The building is more than two centuries old, with a history as rich as its Classic Lobster Dinner ($49). It was home to the first school in Canada to offer children a free education and then, beginning in 1887, to the Victoria School of Art and Design, later the Nova Scotia College of Art and Design.

The most aggressive promoter of the art school was the Indian-born British writer, educator, activist, and suffragist Anna Leonowens. Already a literary celebrity when she settled here in 1881, she had published *The English Governess at the Siamese Court*, a popular account of her adventures while teaching the children of a Siamese king. Decades after her death in 1915, this book became the basis of a bestselling novel, *Anna and the King of Siam*, and then the Broadway musical, *The King and I*, a TV series, and various movies. After Leonowens left Halifax for Montreal around the turn of the century and the art school found another home, Snow and Company, funeral directors, took over the building and used it in 1912 as a morgue for victims of the *Titanic* disaster, and in 1917 for memorial services for hundreds of Halifax Explosion victims.

The second local oasis to gladden Claiborne's taste buds was Fat Frank's on the north side of Spring Garden Road near the corner of Brunswick Street. Its proprietor was Frank Metzger, a suitably rotund and somewhat mysterious American whose manner often suggested he thought his cooking for Haligonians was like casting pearls before swine. But Claiborne, a gent from Manhattan, found nothing at all to complain about. The table settings, "in crystal, silver and napery" were "a joy to be faced with." The snails and mushrooms on toast were "delectable," and the onion soup "first-rate." Both Frank's turtle steak smothered in capers and paprika sauce, and sweetbreads with ham in another paprika sauce were "tender, excellently seasoned and cooked to perfection."

No one loved Fat Frank's more than Keith Spicer, another out-of-towner with expense accounts. I knew him when we were both urchins at Brown Public School in deepest Toronto, and later watched with more than a little envy as he parlayed his wit, bravado, intelligence, loud mouth, and sunny yet blunt disposition into a fabulous and varied career that included a couple of the most important jobs in the country. Fluently bilingual, he was the feds' first and most outspoken and passionate Commissioner of Official Languages (1970-1977), and sixth chairman of the Canadian Radio-Television and Telecommunications Commission (1989-1996). He was also chairman of the Citizens' Forum on National Unity (1990-1991). This so reflected his personality it was better known simply as "the Spicer Commission," and its 168-page conclusion as the "Spicer Report."

Before, between, and after his government jobs, he taught at leading universities not only in Canada but also in the U.S. and Paris. He also squeezed into his furiously energetic life a redoubtable career in French and English print and broadcast journalism. I might have resented his muscling in on my line of work but, in 1985, he popped up as editor-in-chief of the *Ottawa Citizen* and, while turning it into one of the best newspapers in Canada, bought for it a weekly "words" column in which I ridiculed and cursed bureaucrats, academics, politicians, ad writers, and others for mauling and misusing our beautiful English language. "I think your column is fantastic," he told me in a letter, "the best I've ever seen anywhere." This man was obviously beyond reproach.

Whenever business brought Keith to Halifax, he insisted we get together at Fat Frank's. While downing, say, Roast Bore in Madeira Sauce, or Escargot & Lobster Thermidor, which *Where to Eat in Canada* pronounced "superb," we seldom discussed anything more important than the different pig-tailed girls we each adored in grade eight. I do remember, however, that it was at Frank's that he offered me a job for which I was no more qualified than I was for climbing up the outside of the Empire State Building. With his enormous self-confidence he had become so good at making compelling speeches without even glancing at a note that he'd founded a business to teach others how to do it. He called this enterprise Winging It and established branches across much of Canada. So how would I like to open and head up a Winging It office in Halifax? I declined. Keith soon sold the business for a million dollars, and wrote *The Winging It Logic System*.

He wrote eleven books, including his terrific biography, *Life Sentences* (2005). Author and freelance journalist Martin O'Malley called it "a wise, funny book and a glorious read," adding, "I've never met a braver, more ideologically principled, more Canadian Canadian than this man Spicer." Reviewing it in *The Globe and Mail*, Roy McGregor, himself one of Canada's most skilled and prolific authors, said Spicer had "long been our great national dreamer – in both official languages, of course – and his wild optimism for all things Canadian is matched only by his love for this sometimes impossible country."

That love had sprouted as far back as our times together on the big cinder playground at Brown school. Remembering Victory in Europe Day, when he was eleven, he wrote in *Life Sentences*, "As an impressionable, scuff-kneed boy in short pants, I knew already that Canada was an astonishing and privileged place."

It takes me eight years to overcome enough of my sourness about Halifax to begin to appreciate its rare mixture of charm, romance, physical drama, and social intimacy. Jogging here in 1979, I know I'm jogging in My Town. Every step of the way. On summer Sundays, I run past stately wooden rooming houses and the shaded stone mansions of the rich, and then under skyscraping pines while I round the oceanside perimeter of Point Pleasant Park. Big sloops and ketches scoot out to sea and, when they tack, I hear the thunder and flutter of their sails. Seagulls glide and squawk and, on my way back inland, a lawyer sticks his head out his car window and yells, "Drive 'er, Harry, drive 'er."

I drive 'er till I reach the enormous cast-iron gates at the Public Gardens, and then slow down. Ahh, the Gardens. They're the horticulturist's answer to the stately homes of England. Women cruise the curly paths with baby carriages and if those mothers were only nannies with longer skirts, you'd swear the Gardens had whisked you back to Victorian London.

Jogging, however, is illegal in there. I plunge on to Camp Hill graveyard. Halifax has so many downtown cemeteries that, in a play I wrote for CBC Radio, I used real gravestone inscriptions to tell the history of "this old, raw, bloody, greedy, devious, brave, beloved little city by the sea." The play ends with its narrator urging, "Stand here with your feet in the spongy soil of this slightly sunken grave and just listen to the poor, doomed, fleeting city in its glorious, headlong, impertinent celebration of its flicker in time." He was alone in Camp Hill graveyard, now my jogging goal.

By the time I get there, I've done six miles. My torso glistens with sweat, and my face feels as though it must look like a baked tomato. But not far from the grave of statesman Joseph Howe, a faucet sticks out of the ground and a green watering can sits beside it. I fill up the can and dump cold water on my head, four times. What a delicious flicker of time! I walk home, feeling smug. My town.

Owing to our having moved in '73 from our desolate outpost on Prospect Bay to York Street in the heart of the Halifax peninsula, the walk takes only fifteen minutes. It's also a fifteen-minute walk from our house to the Waegwoltic Club, where we all swim in a saltwater lido and our swift day-sailer tugs at her mooring. It's a fifteen-minute walk from home to the office, with its elegant, turn-of-the century fireplace, where I edit *Atlantic Insight* magazine; to the library at Dalhousie University, which I mine for articles I write; the Dalhousie Faculty Club, where I sometimes dine with the urbane; the university track, where I do my most serious running; and the Rebecca Cohn Auditorium, which is not only home to a good film society and symphony orchestra, but also where Penny and I witness performers from the divine (Luciano Pavarotti, Dizzy Gillespie) to the ridiculous (Victor Borge). And then walk home on streets where the heavy branches of a wet night may hang so low the leaves tickle and sprinkle our heads.

It takes all of twenty minutes to stroll downtown to CBC Radio, where I earn a few bucks; to the cozy Halifax Press Club, where I spend a few; to the recently opened Fat's Frank and Five Fishermen, where I spend a few more; to the Neptune Theatre, where the renowned English actor John Neville serves as artistic director and brings new joy to the city's old core of theatre lovers; to the ferries that still chug across the harbour to Dartmouth and, at twenty cents a trip, remain one of North America's sightseeing bargains; to Historic Properties, the renovated pier that's now a cluster of pricey shops and bustling drinking establishments; or, for that matter, to the whole central Halifax waterfront. It's now shedding the moldy, grubby, forlorn look that generations of neglect gave it and slowly emerging as a breezy network of pavilions, restaurants, a marine museum, and eventually even condos.

After I park beside a meter this guy sees me vainly searching my pockets for change, smiles, presses two dimes on me, and keeps on walking. Such incidents doubtless happen in other cities but, nevertheless, I think of him as a classic Halifax man, formal but not stuffy, helpful but not pushy, friendly but never intrusive. He's a stranger, but one who appreciates that we are fellow Haligonians. Halifax is full of people like that. They make you glad to see them, but also respect your space.

If you were to walk down a sleepy Halifax street around breakfast time some golden October morning, and if your eyes met those of a man putting out garbage or a woman raking yellow leaves, it would be unthinkable not to say, "Good morning," or maybe, "Beautiful day, eh?" Since I began to edit *Atlantic Insight*, strangers have stopped me in the street to say, "I really like your magazine." Once, when our sailboat edged close to the backyards of houses on the Northwest Arm, a woman walked out on her pier to tell me the same thing. After I briefly appeared on CBC TV while accepting a national award for a radio play I wrote, I got notes of congratulations, not from other writers, but from neighbours.

All this sounds as though I like Halifax because it massages my ego, and that's partly true. Here, I have become a recognizable frog in a medium-sized pond but the real point is, so is almost everyone else. There are few ciphers among Haligonians; almost everybody is a somebody. The city is gossip-ridden, and this is tribute to its ceaseless fascination with so many of its somebodies. People don't limit their gossip to their separate professions or social enclaves. It ranges freely over who's doing what in the arts, sports, courts, business, media, bureaucracies, real estate, and, always, politics. The talk is proof of the city's life, and my ability to share it.

I love the smell in high summer of the early morning wind in Point Peasant Park. It's full of both carefully cultivated grass and trees, and the wild, clean ocean. The tame and the forever untamable come together in that air, sweeten one another, and remind me that the city has always been an effort to prettify a skinny point of rock that the murdering sea surrounds. It was the exceptionally long and deep harbour, and its strategic location, that inspired England to found Halifax, and the Atlantic still shapes its character, keeps its pride of history fresh, and day and night tells its residents they're all oceanside people.

On every fine weekend from June to deep October, hundreds upon hundreds of Haligonians show up on Sailors Memorial Way in Point Pleasant Park. They come to see and sniff the ocean, to walk, run, and play beside it, and to picnic within earshot of its foamy arrival among beach stones. While giddy dogs race around the green swards, Frisbees whiz among the young, babies snooze in prams, and elderly couples offer seeds to squirrels and chickadees, a colossal ship emerges from the southern horizon, and keeps on coming. It's bound for the container pier beside the lower entrance to the park. This one vessel will enlarge the mountain of truck-sized containers there by several thousand.

Out of curiosity one stormy Saturday in February, I drive the twenty-six miles out to Peggy's Cove and, once there, find gale-force gusts tearing all across those vast stretches of barren and barest rock. Dozens of men and women are already here, standing not far from the lighthouse, shivering in overcoats and parkas, and briefly turning their backs against the pushiest blasts. These people have come out from the city to gaze in wonderment at the giant breakers that furiously thump the granite slopes, and hurl skyward white explosions of spray.

Home of what's surely the world's most photographed lighthouse, Peggy's Cove attracts nearly half a million visitors a year from a dozen nations, but in midwinter few are from further away than Halifax. Haligonians are the major reason that the Sou'Wester

Restaurant manages to stay open out there year-round. Bolted to an outside wall of the lighthouse, incidentally, a weather-worn metal sign displays a wonderfully archaic-sounding message: WARNING. INJURY AND DEATH HAVE REWARDED CARELESS SIGHT-SEERS HERE. THE OCEAN AND ROCKS ARE TREACHEROUS. SAVOUR THE SEA FROM A DISTANCE. Those who've been so horribly rewarded have generally come from far away. Since Haligonians already know enough to stand well out of reach of the rogue waves that sweep tourists to their death at Peggy's Cove, they don't really need the warning. Nor do they need to be told to savour the sea.

If I'd stayed in Toronto, I'd never have discovered that little old Halifax prepared the soil for the very sprouting of Canada. It was from here that in 1758 the Royal Navy transported British troops, one of whose senior officers was Brigadier General James Wolfe, to their conquest of Fortress Louisburg on Cape Breton Island. That victory was a gigantic leap toward the smashing of French power throughout North America. For it cleared the way for the Royal Navy in 1759 to carry British forces, now under the supreme command of Wolfe, up the St. Lawrence, and on to their even greater triumph in the Battle of the Plains of Abraham at Québec City.

As the American Revolution got rolling less than two decades later, rebel forces captured Montreal and attacked Québec, but since support for their cause remained feeble in what was now a French-speaking British colony, they had no choice but to withdraw. Meanwhile, with Halifax calling the shots, Nova Scotia, which included all of the future New Brunswick, refused to join the rebel states. West of Montreal loomed a wilderness shared by aboriginals and a few coureurs de bois. If Nova Scotia had swung over to the rebellion, would it and the future New Brunswick have become American states with the Stars and Stripes as their national flag? Would we have had Donald Trump as our head of state? Would a Canada minus the Maritimes have come into existence? Would a Canada of any kind have come into existence?

Nova Scotia's decision to remain a British colony made it irresistible to roughly 30,000 people who, rather than become citizens of the U.S.A., vowed to continue living under the Union Jack. In 1783-84, these United Empire Loyalists, also known as the "King's Loyal Americans," swamped the local population. They were the down-east wave of a Loyalist migration so huge that Britain not only carved out of Nova Scotia the new colony of New Brunswick, but divided Québec into the colonies of Upper and Lower Canada. British North America was now destined to become predominantly English-speaking. In *True Blue: The Loyalist Legend* (1985), my friend Walter Stewart, head of the journalism school at the University of King's College in the mid-1980s, called the arrival of the Loyalists "the pivotal event in Canadian history."

By the early 1800s, when the future Toronto, "Muddy York," was little more than seventy cabins, four hundred people, and a puny wooden fort, Halifax was the bastion of British power in North America, a bustling, international port of 10,000 residents, boasting architectural treasures like Government House, the Old Town Clock, and St. Paul's Church. It had three newspapers, crowded theatres, a taste for balls, banquets, fireworks, and parades, and a reputation as the home of beautiful, bejewelled, and fashionably dressed women.

Certain Canadian historians have written about the War of 1812 as though Halifax had nothing to do with it but, while American troops were burning York in 1813, Bluenose privateers were terrorizing U.S. ports, and hauling booty – scores of captured, cargo-laden Yankee vessels – into the masted harbour below Citadel Hill. In the summer of 1814, partly in retaliation for the destruction of York, British forces, under Major General Robert Ross, burned down much of Washington, including the Capitol. While leading a later campaign to capture Baltimore, Ross was killed by an American sharpshooter. Preserving his body in a barrel of Jamaican rum, the British shipped it to downtown Halifax in September for interment with full military honours in the Old Burying Ground.

The final and lasting defeat of Napoleon occurred at the Battle of Waterloo on June 18, 1815, and several weeks later, when the fabulous news finally completed its journey across the Atlantic to reach Halifax, ecstasy raced from street to street. The blam-blam of cannon fire echoed up and down the harbour. A grand military review strutted its stuff. A regimental band pumped out patriotic music from a waterfront roof, and in every inn crowds guzzled and gorged, and cheered on happy speechifiers. As night fell, the general "illumination" began. Lighted candles appeared in the windows of every house in the entire city, and the street parties rolled on till nearly dawn.

A part of me still loves what Hog Town school-teachers once taught every little Torontonian to call "The Queen City," and there's no denying its later emergence as one of the best big cities in the world. But for heroes, scoundrels, adventurers, and buccaneers of the past, for swashbuckling, sea-faring, and war-faring in the age of sail, it doesn't come within a nautical mile of Halifax. And later history? Well, there were merely the shipment to Halifax in 1912 of 209 bodies of those who drowned when the *Titanic* went down, and the burial here of 150 of them; the Halifax Explosion, which killed some 2,000 townsfolk in 1917, and remained the world's biggest man-made blast until the atomic bomb obliterated Hiroshima in 1945; and World War II. No city in Canada felt the deprivation, horror, excitement, and thunder of that war more than Halifax. No city was more "in the war," or aroused so much affection and loathing among soldiers and sailors from across the country, or endured anything like the vicious VE Day riots that disgraced the Royal Canadian Navy and wrecked much of our downtown.

More than half a century later, with the twenty-first century fast approaching, Anthony De Palma, *The New York Times*'s bureau chief in Canada, and a writer astute enough to feel exactly as I feel about Halifax, called it "this grand city of the Atlantic," and eloquently explained its grandeur: "I have visited many of the great seaports, and Halifax is alone in North America. It is far more authentic than the totally recreated South Street Seaport in New York. It is more active with commercial liners, container ships and brightly painted lobster boats than the port of Miami. And with the great, gray frigates and hulking submarines of NATO often lining the piers, is just as brawny as the harbour of San Diego without the California cuteness."

Ah yes, those great gray frigates. Well said, Anthony. Long may your big jib draw.

7

That Bounding Main

Our black cat was a come-from-away from Upper Canada for his entfire sixteen years and, although no pet could possibly have been more deeply loved by humans, we somehow never got around to calling him anything more imaginative than Pussy. Before leaving Newcastle, we decided that, as an acknowledgment of both his importance and our destination, we would name him Chedabucto, but somehow that never caught on. We had a similar problem naming sailboats.

The first of our four, a British-built Drascombe Lugger, was unlike any we'd ever seen before. She was just shy of nineteen feet long, just over six wide, and open like a big dory. The hull looked as though it had been constructed with wide wooden lapstrakes, giving the boat stability and an old-fashioned look, but it was actually solid fibreglass in a deep turquoise colour. The topsides were high and the gunwales teak.

She had enough hidden polyurethane foam to make her unsinkable, a well at the stern for an outboard motor, and three reddish-brown sails in a yawl rig. The mainsail was loose-footed (like the others) to prevent accidental gybes from knocking anyone overboard.

Based on the design of small fishing vessels in the choppy English Channel, the Lugger was renowned for her safe, "sea-kindly" performance in rough weather. For messing about in shallow waters she had a pair of sturdy oars and, with the steel centreboard pulled all the way up, a draft of barely ten inches. As *Small Boats Monthly* declared, "We think the Drascombe Lugger is one of the most versatile small boats ever built." Irresistible. We had a new one tugging at her mooring in Prospect Bay within weeks of our arrival here in 1971 and, since Luggers had been in production only since '69, ours may well have been the first in eastern Canada.

But what to call her? For a full year, she was just *Boaty*. So we had Pussy and *Boaty*, but then one clear night in our second summer, while she lay at anchor off our place on Chedabucto Bay, a full moon created a perfect shadow of her floating there in a path of glittering light. Our ten-year-old daughter Annabel, a fan of British singer-songwriter Cat Stevens, and particularly his hit "Moonshadow," looked out from our cottage on the cliff and said, "Look, there it is. It's *Moonshadow*."

Our favourite sail in those days took us about four miles south of our home mooring on the upper reaches of Prospect Bay. We'd pass a couple of barren islands and the picture-perfect Prospect fishing village, and then cross a short stretch of the open Atlantic to a maze of little cliffs, rocky crags, granite headlands, and deserted isles. Known as Rogues Roost, this inshore wilderness, with its narrows and sheltered coves, long served as a hideout for the vessels of rum-runners, pirates, and privateers. For us, however, its most precious asset was a clean, tiny, crescent-shaped beach in a cove where the water had a Caribbean colour and clarity.

One brilliant Sunday afternoon, when the breeze in there was soft, we hauled down our mainsail, let the two others idly luff, and prepared to row to the beach, pull our bow up on the sand, and unpack our picnic. Just then, a long, open, wooden boat with an inboard engine tore out at us from behind an island to the east. Her skipper, a scowling, middle-aged man, spun her expertly abeam of us, and his young crewman, probably his son, grabbed ours by the port gunwale, and held it against their boat. The older fellow joined him, peered fiercely up and down the interior of ours, and growled a question I couldn't understand. His accent was thick, and as baffling as his alarming arrival.

I felt as though we'd somehow sailed into a strange country, but then it dawned on me that he was a lobster fisherman from nearby Terence Bay or Lower Prospect and that, since *Moonshadow* from a distance looked more like a workboat to him than a yacht, he suspected we were lobster poachers.

Once he realized we weren't, he looked a bit guilty, and shyly shoved an open bottle of rum at me. I took a swig but, forgetting I'd slathered my lips with zinc oxide to protect them from sun blisters, I handed it back to him with white guck smeared all around its neck. He looked at it for just a second and, apparently thinking it would be insulting to wipe the stuff off, drank from the bottle as it was, lifted it in a kind of farewell salute, and tore off in the direction he'd come.

On another Sunday, with a stiff wind charging up Prospect Bay from the southwest, Penny and I hired a babysitter and sailed down past Prospect and out towards Hearn Island. West of Rogues Roost, it was bigger than any of the islands we knew over there and more exposed to the open Atlantic.

Even in the lee of the island, the wind was stronger than any we'd ever handled before, and close-hauled on a port tack we romped westward on a ride so thrilling it kept us hollering and whooping. But once past the island, with nothing to windward except the tempestuous Atlantic, things got downright scary. The wind felt like a gale and our bow spray like buckets of water thrown in our faces. The waves were just too damn big and the breakers too violent. We pulled abreast of a big ketch. She was more than forty feet long but, for safety's sake, her crew had hauled down the mainsail to let just the smaller jib and mizzen drive her.

We should have lowered our own main but felt safer spilling wind from it, carefully turning to starboard and running back up Prospect Bay to our mooring. When I was eighty-one I stumbled on a story that made me thankful indeed that, more than four decades earlier, we had headed for home when we did.

In heavy weather and icy water off West Cork, Ireland, a Lugger with two men and a woman aboard was capsized by an accidental gybe, and immediately turned turtle. The centreboard slammed back into its casing and that meant that, although the boat was floating, no one could right her. One man and the woman managed to swim to an island, but the Lugger's sixty-six-year-old owner, a highly experienced sailor, "died of acute cardiac failure due to drowning and hypothermia." Whether out at sea, on a mirror-calm lake, or in a cozy harbour, no sailboat is ever immune to the unpredictable.

Our next boat was from Sweden. Here I am in Canada's number one province for seagoing history, home of the builders of both the *Bluenose* and *Bluenose II*, the reproduction of HMS *Bounty* for the Hollywood movie *Mutiny on the Bounty*, Cape Islander fishing boats, wooden pleasure schooners, and countless fibreglass dinghies, daysailers, and cruising yachts of proven local design and superior craftsmanship and, having bought one sailboat from a yard in Britain, I now ordered a bigger one from a yard on a lake in the middle of Sweden.

This was an Albin Vega, a 27-foot-long, eight-foot-wide, sloop-rigged cruiser with a Volvo diesel engine, and the speed, manageability, and seaworthiness that had already enabled Vegas to make transatlantic crossings and would later see one sail on a single voyage around both North and South America, and another circumnavigate the whole world. In photos of a Vega's interior, I could see the soft, blue, full-length berths, stainless-steel galley equipment, and hand-rubbed mahogany and teak table that at lunchtime in, say, English Harbour, Antigua, I could lift out of our cabin and set up in the cockpit. Under full sail the Albin Vega looked businesslike yet beautiful, efficient yet romantic. She had a certain European flavour, a joie de vivre about her, and I hadn't a whiff of doubt that we were made for each other. Penny and I paid roughly $26,000 for her (equivalent to $144,000 in 2020 currency).

She arrived at the South End Container Terminal one sunny day in June 1974, but due to some hitch in import procedures, we could not take possession of her for nearly two weeks. Her topsides were a gorgeous, brilliant, and deepest rosy red, and she just sat out there on a cradle about a hundred yards from the locked gate of the terminal, all by her spectacular self, and every day we showed up with binoculars just to gasp at her fabulous beauty.

Moonshadow's Halifax mooring had been with the other small centreboard boats at the Waegwoltic, but we chose to keep the Vega among the scores of keelboats at the Armdale Yacht Club. With the assistance of Albin Marine's agent here, we finally collected her from the container pier, had her delivered to the club, stepped her mast, got her all ready to go, and, as the sun sank, launched her. We had no launching ceremony. We just couldn't quite see anyone solemnly declaring, "I hereby name this ship *Boaty*. May God bless her and all who sail on her." Nor did Penny and I dare to do anything as risky as take her out for a sail. We just went aboard, lovingly stroked everything from cabin top to floorboards, from sink to winches and bulwark to births, and then, giddy with joy, sat in her cockpit and downed a picnic banquet: fresh crabmeat sandwiches with chilled Pouilly-Fuissé, and Stilton with Taylor Fladgate tawny port.

The next day, the diesel engine in *Boaty* refused to start and, since I lacked the confidence to sail her without auxiliary power to fall back on, she stayed at her mooring for the entire three weeks that it took a repairman to get and install a new part the engine required. But then, under full sail with our whole family aboard, *Boaty* repeatedly charged down the Arm, past the coves to starboard – Ferguson's, Herring, Portuguese, and Duncan's – and sometimes all the way out to the oldest working lighthouse in North America, the one on Sambro Island. In every kind of wind, light, spotty, brisk, steady, and from no matter what direction, she handled easily and sailed flawlessly.

Even the diesel worked smoothly. We rarely turned it on but while tacking up the Arm on one of our earliest outings, I took *Boaty* too close to the shore opposite the Royal Nova Scotia Yacht Squadron, nudged her keel on a submerged rock, and briefly used the engine to back her into deeper water. This all took no more than a few seconds but several days later, an annoying guy at the Armdale said, "Hey, Harry, I heard you ran aground across from the Squadron. How the heck did you do that?"

This reminded me of an unpleasant tendency among yacht club members that I'd first discovered in Toronto: if you make a stupid mistake with your boat, the odds are extremely high that some yachter will witness it, delight in it, and immediately broadcast the news. The rule would soon apply to me and *Boaty* once again, only this time in the most spectacular fashion possible.

I blame what happened entirely on W.O. Mitchell. The author of the novel *Who Has Seen the Wind*, which since its publication in 1947 has racked up sales of almost a million copies, he visited Halifax in the summer of 1975. Critics still saw *Who Has Seen the Wind* as a masterpiece, and Mitchell had since written two more novels, a stage play, and six years of CBC's beloved weekly radio show, *Jake and the Kid*. He had also blossomed as a performer on stage, screen, and radio and, for all these reasons, he arrived here as that rarest of creatures, a Canadian literary celebrity.

During Peter Gzowski's long, shining career as the host of CBC radio talk shows, no one was a more reliable guest than Mitchell. Seat him near any microphone and away he'd go. His wit was quick, delivery flawless, and supply of hilarious yarns and memories inexhaustible. In *Stories About Storytellers* (2011), his editor, Douglas Gibson, remembered, "His performances were immaculately professional: voice husking or thundering, fist raised, white hair flying, mouth creased in a foxy grin, or eyes wide in innocent astonishment at a double entendre raising a laugh ... He himself was perhaps the most outrageous character he ever created."

Speaking of outrageous characters, Farley Mowat was totally immune to Mitchell's charm. Not a man to let the sale of more than 14 million copies of his thirty-nine books, or the passage of half a century, annul a grudge, Mowat, in his late seventies, told me that at nineteen he'd submitted a short story to *Maclean's* but that Mitchell, the fiction editor there, had rejected it and – stupid, miserable arsehole that he was – told him that if he wanted to sell fiction to *Maclean's* he'd better learn to write about "boy-meets-girl-boy-gets-girl." (My father's story, "The Wind in the Juniper," which ran in *Maclean's* during Mitchell's reign as fiction editor, must have done an end run around this formula. It was inspired by the death from accidental radiation poisoning, at Los Almos National Laboratory in New Mexico, of Canadian nuclear scientist Louis Slotin.)

But back to Mitchell and *Boaty*. I loved *Who Has Seen the Wind* myself, and believed my father and he had deeply respected each other's writing. Moreover, I had discovered, probably during one of Peter's interviews with Mitchell, that he and Merna were addicted to sailing an eighteen-foot sloop on a lake in Alberta. Who better to take out on the Atlantic in our splendid new *Boaty* than this laureate of the Prairies and his creative partner?

By early one fine, sunny Saturday afternoon in mid-August then, Penny, Merna, and Annabel were sitting in the cockpit, and Alec stood ready to cast off at the bow. Mitchell and I were also up forward. I had pulled the jib out of its bag and was attaching its leading edge to the forestay. When I'd finished, and secured the highest of the sail's three corners to the halyard line, Penny, still in the cockpit, would haul on her end of the line until the sail was completely raised and then secure it to a cleat. Up forward, I'd now grab the jib and hold it in the right position for the wind to fill it and push *Boaty*'s bow in a direction away from the uncomfortably close shore. At the right second, Alec would let the mooring line go, and off we'd sail with Penny handling the tiller.

That, at least, is how things had worked a dozen times before, and I felt pretty good knowing how to leave the mooring without using our engine. The mooring happened to be within what the Honourable Isadore LeBlanc, when in good order, would have seen as no more than pissing distance from the Armdale's clubhouse. Outside the second-floor restaurant, a deck offered splendid views of the Arm in the distance and *Boaty* at close range. A dozen or so members of the club and their guests, most of them, in my memory, swigging Schooner lager, sat up there idly watching our preparations. *Boaty* was not only sensationally red, but the newest keelboat at an Armdale mooring.

I was trying to concentrate on the job at hand but Mitchell pushed his face so close to mine I couldn't see past it and, with his arms waving around and his voice husking and thundering, shouted zany stories. Back on *Gazette*, I'd have liked nothing better, but the last thing I needed now was this "most outrageous character" right in my face and, sure enough, when Penny raised the jib, it was flawlessly fixed to the forestay – but upside down!

The beer-drinkers above burst into laughter. I had secured the halyard to the foremost lower corner of the sail and thereby given them this spectacular pratfall to gloat over. Luckily, Alec still had a good grip on the mooring line. We soon got the jib up properly, left our audience behind, sailed briskly down the Arm, and revelled in a glorious sail well out in the ocean.

For the rest of the sailing season in '74, and from early June to late October of '75, we repeatedly sailed *Boaty* for miles beyond Point Pleasant Park and then back to her mooring. The more we sailed her the more I loved her, but a certain financial reality gradually undermined my pleasure.

I had sunk so much money into buying *Boaty* that I'd fallen dangerously behind in paying my income tax. On fine sailing days, I'd be writing in the sweaty, third-floor office of our house on York Street and, especially if I'd run into rough going up there, I'd think, Hey, I spent all that money on *Boaty* and I'm not even sailing her. So we'd sail south until the tallest buildings in Halifax looked like a few little spikes astern, and then I'd start fretting, Hey, if I don't churn out more writing

I can sell, I'll never be able to pay what I owe Canada Revenue. Back up the Arm we'd fly. In the sweaty office, the old black Underwood stood at the ready.

By the spring of '76, Penny and I decided to forgo sailing until after the couple of weeks it might take for us to get back on our feet financially but, as late as August, *Boaty* remained where she'd been all winter, high, dry, and conspicuous in the Armdale's yard. She was little more than two years old, in flawless condition, and all by herself among the scores of empty cradles left behind by boats launched for the season back in June. One sunny Sunday, Alec was proudly brushing creamy anti-fouling paint on her keel when a middle-aged man, sniffing a possible bargain, said, "Tell me, son, has the owner of this boat passed away?"

That triggered a decidedly unadventurous line of thought. Even after sailing *Boaty* such a short time, I suspected that, for as long as we had her, she'd be gobbling money for not only routine maintenance and yacht club services, but also to pay for nasty surprises like torn-apart sails, gouged topsides, engine break-downs, and broken rigging. For yachts, everything from that anti-fouling paint to deck hardware, from wax to turnbuckles to teak oil always costs more than you think it will. In the early 1900s, the British tea and grocery tycoon Sir Thomas Lipton was racing gorgeous sloops more than one hundred feet long, and I had now begun to grasp the full meaning of his reply to inquiries about the cost of looking after one of those giant beauties: "If you have to ask, you can't afford it."

I knew zilch about auxiliary engines or power tools. The only tool I'd ever handled skillfully was a typewriter, manual, not much use while restoring faded fibreglass to its deep colour and rich shine. That was only one of countless yacht-maintenance jobs I would probably never get around to mastering. I loved sailing, but not applying elbow grease to sailboats.

From yachting magazines and seasoned Armdale sailors, I gathered that after owning *Boaty* for a few more years, we'd find that the annual cost of having her properly maintained would run to maybe 10 percent of her original purchase price, or $2,600 ($11,000 in 2019). In those days, that would pay a whack of tuition fees. Meanwhile, our children were fifteen, thirteen, and eight, and did we really want to pack them into *Boaty* and sail some two thousand miles down through the stormy North Atlantic, across the Bermuda Triangle, and further south to Antigua, where they could eat lunch on the table I'd pulled out of our cabin and set up in the cockpit? Nope.

Thus it was that, after owning this *Boaty* only since the spring of '74 and sailing her for all of two seasons without ever taking her far enough to spend a night aboard, we sold her in the fall of '76 for very close to what we'd paid for her. Fair thee well, *Boaty*, and may the wind always be at your back or, better still, abeam.

The buyer, a keen sailor of centreboard boats in his thirties, with a wife and a couple of children, seemed exceptionally happy to get *Boaty*, and to start making her an important part of their lives together. Glimpsing her occasionally in the Arm over the next couple of decades, I always felt a twinge of regret but also, as though she were a beloved water spaniel we'd had to give up, a certain relief that her owners were kind and caring.

Back in '78, only two years after the sale, that

master storyteller, W.O. Mitchell, made sure my most embarrassing experience with her came back to haunt me. He and I found ourselves seated among eight diners at one of dozens of round tables in the cavernous banquet hall of a four-star hotel in Toronto. The event was the annual awards night of the Association of Canadian and Television and Radio Artists, and I was there because I was on the short list for the prize for the best radio play written in English.

My tablemates, aside from Mitchell, were seemingly modest TV producers and solemn CBC executives, all of whom he decided needed entertainment from him. So he regaled them with a story about how that fellow right there, Harry Bruce, this "expert" sailor from the home province of legendary sea dogs, had tried to go sailing in his spanking new yacht – with the jib upside down. Ha, ha. This happened not in Halifax, but Lunenburg. The audience consisted not of members of any yacht club, but of grizzled Lunenburg cod fishermen, wearing rubber boots and black, sou'wester rain hats. Oh well, at least I brought home the radio-play award.

Among the boats we bought in Halifax, *Boaty* was the only one with a permanent keel. Her successor was a racy, seventeen-foot, self-bailing, centreboard sloop that the Boston Whaler company built, and marketed as the Harpoon. The firm was famous for its light, tough, and unsinkable motorboats, and the unshakable loyalty of those who bought them. This was a company that, by all accounts, had never sold a bummer, and its salesman in Halifax was an Englishman who'd been a competitive dinghy sailor in his homeland.

To prove the virtues of the Harpoon, one breezy

afternoon he invited me to join him on one for a brief, thrilling romp on the Arm. While I was handling the jib, and he the mainsail and tiller, he showed me a trick I'd never thought possible. Having turned the main over to me for a few seconds, he kept the tiller in his left hand while, with his right, he tied a bowline knot. Yes, he actually tied a flawless bowline with just one hand. Surely it would have been foolish not to buy whatever craft an expert like that recommended, and such is the logic of anyone who's hot to buy a lovely new sailboat.

I best remember our Harpoon for a fabulous sail beyond the Arm with my old friend, Kildare Dobbs, and a deeply humiliating sail within the Arm with my young son, Max. Kildare was an Anglo-Irish but mostly Canadian author of books of essays, poems, short stories, memoirs, travel writing, and satiric history. He won both a Governor General's Award for Non-fiction and myriad literary friends, including novelists Mordecai Richler and Brian Moore, and poet Richard Greene. "He was a superb prose stylist and a very good poet," Greene said. "He was an outstanding publisher and mentor to many writers … the last great voice of a generation of Canadian writers that now falls silent."

I knew him as a rumpled, baldish, blondish, soft-spoken man, maybe a bit overweight, with a trace of the English gent in his accent. He had a sly sense of humour, an endless supply of stories about writers, and a generosity of spirit that, together, made him the most convivial man I ever shared a bottle of gin with. At eighty-seven, right after the publication of his *Casanova in Venice: A Raunchy Rhyme*, he told an interviewer that he now hoped to write a book of playful rhymes about drinking. Yeats, Auden, and Omar Khayam, he said, had all written verse about drinking. He would call his collection The Happy Hour. Alas, he died at eighty-nine, before he could finish it. The longer he'd lived the less often we got together and, remembering him now, I think of a bottle of fine red wine. The longer it remained uncorked the more its taste improved; the longer my friendship with Kildare remained unrefreshed by our seeing each other, the more I treasured it.

Middle-aged, desk-ridden, and somewhat puffy, seated side by side on the narrow, windward deck of the Harpoon and trying to keep her flat while a tough beam wind thwacked her sails, Kildare and I leaned backward over the water as far as we dared. He controlled the jib, and I the mainsail and tiller, and on this absolutely splendid afternoon for saltwater sailing in August 1979 we tore down the Arm to the widening harbour and, beyond that, the corrugated horizon of the open ocean.

Coming back as well, we flew along on a beam reach. At one point, when the waves, wind, and our momentum combined in just the right way, the boat began to "plane." She rose up and rode on her bow wave at seemingly miraculous speed. Planing, by then, was routine for young athletes who sailed light centreboard craft in international competition, but neither Kildare nor I had ever experienced it. It was the high point in an afternoon of unforgettable exultation.

The low point in an afternoon of unforgettable stupidity occurred while I was trying to teach eleven-year-old Max that the heeling of a sailboat was nothing to worry about. I capsized the Harpoon with him on board. This was a truly spectacular demonstration of father knows worst. Unlike Alec and Annabel, both seemingly born sailors, Max suffered a flood of panic the moment any sailboat he was aboard began to heel. Feeling that no son of mine should be doomed to go through life without loving sailing, I decided to cure him.

I took him out on the Harpoon and soon, just off the Dingle, began to sail close to the wind with the board down. I told him exactly why she was heeling a bit and then, just to show him how safe it was to make her heel over more, I headed off wind a smidgeon and yanked the mainsail in. But I failed either to realize how tender the Harpoon was or to spot the looming assault of a nasty gust of wind, or both. Oops! Over she went.

All I can remember about the horrifying confusion of the next split seconds was that, finding myself dumped in shockingly cold water, I reached up to grab the overturned hull, failed to see my son anywhere, desperately screamed, "Max!" plunged headfirst back underwater to free him from whatever had trapped him down there, again saw no sign of him, hurled myself back into the air – and there he was, calmly riding the overturned hull. As the boat had gone over, he had so quickly and nimbly spun himself onto the floating hull that most of his body and all of his curly hair were still dry. To this day, when he is fifty-two and a computer-animation expert for Hollywood movies, I have no idea why I hadn't seen him earlier.

With Max perched on the upturned hull, I bobbed around in the water, grabbed the boat now and then, fretted over what to do next, and just got colder and colder. A Coast Guard motor launch finally came to the rescue. The skipper, who had no crew, helped us aboard but, though willing to hang around while I figured out how to right the Harpoon, he had no idea how to use his launch to help me do it. He seemed rather bored.

I hailed a family in a passing cabin cruiser and asked if they'd please deliver Max to the foot of Jubilee Road and, while he trotted up from there to our home on York Street, I was again thrashing around and under the Harpoon. This time, I tried to get a line secured as close as possible to her underwater gunwale and then looped around the boat and over to me as I stood on the centreboard. I'd then haul on the free end until she sat on the water as she should with the mast pointed straight up at the sky. That was the plan anyway, but I was just too damn weak. I was forty-six years old, and the Harpoon nearly eight feet wide.

And then, it happened. My guardian angel emerged from nowhere and floated beside me. He took the line from me, politely ordered me to return to the rescue launch, and, within two minutes, somehow righted the Harpoon by himself. Her sails were soaked, but still raised, and her rudder was still in place. Half-full of water, she wallowed a bit, but when my rescuer scrambled aboard and, under his urging, I followed him, she already seemed ready to go. And so she was. He took control of the tiller and mainsail. I had begun to shiver but managed to handle the jib and, while we arrowed across a couple of hundred yards to the Halifax side of the Arm, the boat's self-bailing system drained her dry.

My rescuer's destination was the private dock at one of those waterfront properties that Halifax multi-millionaires called home, and as soon as we'd dropped the sails and tied up there, he must have decided my clumsiness and fierce shivering were dangerous signs of hypothermia. He led me inside what looked like a boathouse but was actually a little cottage that housed a kind of bedsitting room. He told me to take off my wet shirt and lie down on a single bed, covered me with blankets, and turned on a space heater. Within forty-five minutes, I felt perfectly normal, and more grateful than I could ever put into words.

I can't remember getting home that afternoon, or sailing the Harpoon back to its mooring at the Waegwaltic Club. Nor do I remember how my rescuer had arrived at my side in the water. Had he been picnicking with friends at the nearby Dingle, seen the mess I was in, and swiftly swum out? He was young, maybe nineteen or twenty, lean, tanned, and broad-shouldered, with trim dark hair and a pleasant manner. I never discovered whether he lived at the property where we docked the Harpoon or just knew the owners. Wanting no recognition for his heroism, he wouldn't even give me his name. And Max? Oddly enough, being dumped actually cured him of his fear. Sailing became and remains just an activity in which he has no interest at all.

Our final sailboat in Nova Scotia was our first's big brother: The Drascombe Coaster. She had three rust-coloured, loose-footed sails in a yawl rig, just like the Lugger's, only larger. Her hull and topsides were the same shape as the Lugger's, but at nearly twenty-two feet long, she was quite a bit bigger. The Lugger was entirely open, but the Coaster had a cuddy cabin and, inside that, two full-length berths and a tiny alcohol-burning gadget for cooking. Drawing less than a foot of water with the board up and, with astute reefing, manageable and seaworthy even in gale-force winds, the Coaster was the perfect little family sailboat on Chedabucto Bay, and we happily sailed her there off and on for a dozen summers.

In my mid-sixties, however, the eight-horsepower outboard motor mysteriously put on so much weight I could barely carry it, and the annual cleaning and buffing of the Coaster's hull, and applying the anti-fouling paint, and also the careful oiling of the teak gunwales – these tasks, once such a pleasure, were becoming a sweaty ordeal amidst ever-more-bloodthirsty mobs of black flies. We put her up for sale. A buyer came all the way down from Saint John, looked her over, met our price, and hauled her away.

Goodbye, final *Boaty*, and to sailing, Adieu.

8

High Old Times at The Carleton Hotel

In 1985 I finished *The Man and the Empire: Frank Sobey*, a 443-page biography, and the second of the eight commissioned books that helped me and my family survive in Halifax for more than half my life. Commissioned books are those that a corporation or individual with lots of money pays someone like me to write. The corporation might want a flattering portrait of itself. The individual might want to celebrate between hard covers the life of a beloved parent, sports or movie star, or, most often, a remarkable business leader.

It was Donald, the youngest of supermarket tycoon Frank Sobey's three sons, who paid me to write a biography of his father. One of a handful of legendary business geniuses in the Maritimes, Frank started out helping his father run a butcher shop that peddled its meat door-to-door from a horse-drawn wagon in

Stellarton, Nova Scotia. By the 1980s he'd parlayed that, with the help of his sons, into an empire comprising seventy-five supermarkets in five provinces, plus corner stores, drugstores, wholesaling companies, movie theatres, shopping malls, office buildings, a whack of stock-market investments, and enough leasable space for ninety-two Canadian football fields. (Led by his sons, grandsons, and their chosen executives, Sobeys Inc., is now second only to Loblaws Canada Limited as a Canadian food retailer. It boasts 1,500 stores in all ten provinces and more than 25,000 employees. In its 2019 operating year it landed sales totalling no less than C$25 billion.)

Since writing a commissioned book turns its author into a kind of literary mercenary, a hack who's supposedly happy to write anything for the right price, critics have tended to ignore such works or dismiss them as second-rate or worse. To lessen at least some of this taint, my agreement with Donald specified that he could kill parts of the manuscript that he felt would damage Frank's reputation, but not make me insert anything I saw as favourable guff. This worked well, if I do say so myself. In the Montreal *Gazette*, Hubert Bauch said, "Frank Sobey should be required reading for anyone with dreams of taking a modest venture for a ride into the corporate stratosphere." He went on to describe my prose as "at once lively and smooth" and my "feel for the Maritime pulse" as "unerring."

The most nerve-wracking part of the job had not been the writing but the reading aloud of the finished manuscript to its protagonist. Early in the winter of 1985, Donald assigned me to join Frank in a room at the Chateau Halifax (now the Hotel Halifax) on every weekday until I'd read to him every one of the more than 110,000 words I'd written about him.

At eighty-two, Frank was still so pushy and interrogatory about the daily workings of his Stellarton-based companies that I suspected his sons decided a fine way to get him out of their hair for a while was to have him visit Halifax to hear me tell him all about himself. This, I feared, would be the most painful, minute-by-minute ordeal I'd ever endured as a writer. Would he quibble over the wording in every other sentence, and insist on changes in meaning, insertions of flattering information about himself, and outright deletions? Would I be suffering these sessions day after day after day until springtime?

As it turned out, he demanded only a handful of changes, and they were not about him but the people of his beloved Pictou County. It was wrong, for example, to report that a couple of Stellarton coal miners might get drunk on Saturday night but then, on Monday morning, return to the pits with their arms around each other's shoulders. Pictou County miners, Frank insisted, were the finest people in the world, and did not get drunk. While such complaints were easy enough to handle, I still feared that, at any moment, he'd interrupt me to denounce something I'd just read to him, and it was always with enormous relief that I got out of there at lunchtime.

"Would you like to join me for lunch at The News Room?" he asked as we finished the tenth of my eleven chapters.

"Uh, well, thank you very much, Mr. Sobey, but I'm afraid I've got to meet someone."

"I bet you're going to The Press Club," he said. How in heck did he know about that? The News Room was a good restaurant on the ground floor of the historic Carleton Hotel. The Press Club, in the basement below, was a hangout for journalists and, among others, the civil servants who dealt with them. It had never occurred to me for a moment that Frank had ever heard of it, much less knew where it was. I should have known better. In my own book, a Montreal businessman marvels, "If Frank Sobey lives to be ninety, he'll know everything that's going on at every company in which he's got money." I wasn't a company, but I'd been receiving Sobey money for close to three years.

Back at the Chateau Halifax at two o'clock, I resumed my dreary reading. In shirtsleeves and sock feet, with his tie tossed on a bed, Frank sagged in an armchair, while I started Chapter 11, "The Man, the Empire, the Dynasty." I read like some sort of automaton, and it wasn't until maybe forty-five minutes had passed that I paused and glanced at Frank. Glory be, he was sound asleep! I silently pulled on my overcoat, sneaked my manuscript into my briefcase, and tiptoed to the door. I turned the knob, it clicked, he woke. "Where do you think you're going?" asked the head of the Empire and father of the Dynasty. And I was going nowhere for another couple of hours.

The next day I asked the chatty young maître d' at The News Room if she knew Frank by sight. Yes. And did he have lunch there yesterday? Yes. Well, I was just wondering if he'd had anything alcoholic to drink. Yes again. Two double martinis, extra dry. That would have knocked me out after lunch, and I was three decades younger than him.

Built in 1760, The Carleton is the oldest stone building in Halifax. Also known, during a past both seedy and splendid, as not only The Carleton Hotel but Carleton House, it sits at the southeast corner of Argyle and Prince streets. Its wall on Prince faces the back of the wooden St. Paul's Church. Erected in 1750, just one year after the founding of Halifax and the arrival from Britain of the first Haligonians, St. Paul's is the oldest building in the city, and not only Canada's oldest Anglican church but its oldest Protestant place of worship.

These days, it's The Press Gang that occupies The Carleton's basement. Named after the squads of brutal thugs that, during the building's youth, the Royal Navy sent ashore to snatch men off downtown streets for lifetime enslavement aboard warships, The Press Gang is the priciest restaurant in the city. The ground floor above it offers what one reviewer calls "upscale pub grub," and shows by pop-music bands from all over Canada. The three upper storeys contain kitchen-equipped suites and rooms that, according to some of those brave enough to have rented them, are so loud they're fit only for the stone-deaf. A five-star apartment hotel The Carleton is not.

In the beginning, it was a mansion that a powerful administrator in the colonial government built for himself. He was the Dublin-born Richard Bulkeley who, as the well-heeled thirty-one-year-old aide-de-camp to the first governor of Nova Scotia, Edward Cornwallis, was among those earliest settlers in Halifax. "A healthy, vigorous and hard-working civil servant," historian Phyllis Blakeley wrote, "he assisted 13 governors and lieutenant governors from Cornwallis to

Wentworth. In half a century of service he took part in
not only the founding of Halifax, but the immigration
of New Englanders and Loyalists, and the prosperity
of the French revolutionary wars." He was a man of
"inflexible integrity" and in his obituary was called
"the Father of the Province." As a crippled old cod-
ger, Bulkeley was Judge of the Court of Admiralty, and
held court in his house. In a scuffle between civil and
naval authority in 1798, his forty-ninth year in Halifax,
he summoned nine captains to his private courtroom
and tongue-lashed them for repeatedly and illegally or-
dering press gangs to kidnap locals.

Oddly, Halifax never named a street after this ex-
ceptional come-from-away. Nowhere in town is there
either a "Bulkeley Boulevard" or a statue of him. A
suitable statue would have him raising his glass to toast
the guest of honour at one of his lavish dinner parties.
Known for decades for his extravagant hospitality, he
particularly enjoyed entertaining senior military officers, and James Wolfe was among the earliest. Wolfe
was about to lead the conquest of Louisbourg, and
Bulkeley would be quick to salvage from the ruined
fortress both stones for the walls of his new mansion
and, to adorn one of the rooms, the defeated French
governor's black marble mantel.

Although the residence would eventually be but
one corner of the hotel that encased it, its dining room
alone was big enough to seat fifty. Bulkeley held generous New Year's Day levees at the house, and dinner
parties on both royal birthdays and St. Patrick's and
St. George's days. In 1786, fellow Irishman Guy Carleton, who, a decade earlier, had led the British forces
that kicked the rebel invaders out of Québec, arrived in

Halifax as Baron Dorchester, the new Governor General of all British North America. Bulkeley not only welcomed him to his home, but named it after him.

Among other notable guests that Carleton House pampered were a couple of princes. One was William Henry, the future King William IV. He first arrived in 1784 as a twenty-one-year-old captain in the Royal Navy, and launched a love affair, which he refreshed during subsequent visits, with Lady Frances Wentworth, twice his age and the wife of a future Lieutenant Governor of Nova Scotia. The other prince was William's younger brother, Edward Augustus, Duke of Kent. He settled in Halifax in 1794 as the energetic and brutal disciplinarian who commanded Britain's military forces in Nova Scotia and New Brunswick, and stayed for a half a dozen years. Edward would eventually become the father of Queen Victoria, and William one of her uncles.

By 1908, when Henry Ford boasted that his new Model T was "stronger than a horse and easier to maintain," The Carleton had long been a hotel, and my aunt Anna, then a girl of fifteen, stayed there briefly with her grandmother Tory. Anorah Tory lived near the Bruces in Guysborough County, but loved to visit Halifax and especially the Public Gardens, which looked as British as Big Ben (and still do). The Carleton Hotel, Anna remembered in her own old age, was cozy, quiet, reasonably priced, and, all in all, an entirely suitable place for an elderly lady from the sticks to stay with her teenage granddaughter.

Nearly eight decades after that, Penny and I tried to celebrate our fifteenth year in Halifax by going there on Hallowe'en night and taking a second-floor corner room. It offered a matchless view of the biggest, weirdest, and – for those who hated crowds – most unnerving annual party in all Canada. Close to 40,000 men, women, and teenagers, most of them in bizarre costumes, milled around, squashed against one another, jammed half a dozen bars where the staff sported wild outfits of their own, and screamed their lungs out on two short city blocks.

Penny and I reached our room as early as nine o'clock, but the bedlam had already begun. We poured some rum, toasted Halifax, opened the windows, and let the din roar in from the street. After a while I ventured into the mob below. So close I could have beaned it with a candy kiss loomed the white, wooden backside of St. Paul's, the first Church of England cathedral in all of Britain's overseas colonies. Topping its font was a carved dove with outstretched wings that dated back to the reign of Charles I and witch burnings.

But now, tipsy witches shrieked within a few yards of this "Westminster Abbey of Canada," Lucifers leered, and vampires bared their teeth. Mickey and Minnie Mouses and bees from outer space cavorted on Argyle, with alligators, werewolves, the lion from Oz, abominable snowmen, World War I air aces, roaring Viking warriors, Arthurian knights, Swiss yodellers, Arab sheiks, Dutch dairymaids, Picasso clowns, Emmet Kelly clowns, blinking robots, peaceniks, terrorists, cowboys, convicts, astronauts, sailors, ballplayers, moonies, Mounties, and redcoats like those once seen around here every day.

Monks, Roman senators, Batman, Quasimodo, Don Quixote, Darth Vader, the Planters Peanut Man, a couple of Zorros, and the only Groucho Marx I've ever seen in a red and black lumberjack shirt, they all ogled nuns, belly dancers, geisha girls, the Queen of Hearts, Miss Liberty, a female Paul Revere, two big girls in diapers who sucked on baby bottles, and a dozen witches who'd dressed for seduction rather than flying on broomsticks.

"Did you see the guy with flies all over his face?" a six-foot vampire with a stake in his chest asked a five-foot Charlie Chaplin. "Yeah," Charlie replied, "and what about that dork with his eyeball hanging out?"

"Come on," said a college boy, dressed somewhat like a pirate, "do I look like a mermaid?" He was trying to gaze deeply into the hard eyes of a pretty young woman wearing a short fur coat, hot pants, fishnet stockings, and stiletto heels. "No, honey," she said, "but you don't look like no pirate either." Klondike Kate reeled by, leaning on Merlin, who had a stuffed parrot on his shoulder, and marvelled, "Here I am, hanging onto this man, and I don't even know him."

Raggedy Ann noticed my notebook. "You a reporter?" she demanded. "Yes, I guess so." She waved a hacksaw in my face and asked, "Want your beer opened?" A monstrous Smurf gave three uncostumed teenagers a jolly greeting just as a bottle of rum slipped from one boy's hand and smashed on the pavement. "Fuck off, Smurf," the boy shouted. I'd had enough.

By dangling my key over the heads of the surging mob at the entrance to The Carleton, I informed a bouncer that I had a room there, and he cleared a path through the creatures for me. Upstairs Penny and I closed the windows, but the street noise still filled the room. A baseball fan told me the next day that from half a mile south, the Hallowe'en din from Argyle

Street was like the roar of Yankee Stadium as he'd approached it from blocks away during a World Series Game. I wondered what Bulkeley's ghost thought of this outlandish bust-up, and was glad Aunt Anna, now ninety-three, was not with us. We had planned to spend the night at The Carleton but, while the fantastic spectacle outside strained hard to be happy, it was oddly depressing. We missed our uptown nest. At 2.30 a.m. we picked our way through shards and upchucked spills on Argyle and strolled past a few lonely young drunks, up Spring Garden Road, beside the Public Gardens, and into the neighbourhood of Dalhousie University. By three, we were under the covers in our own bed.

In the early '90s, the Mardi Gras, as we'd seen it, was falling out of favour and into oblivion. City councillor and former mayor Walter Fitzgerald damned it as nothing more than "a drunken brawl," and enough Haligonians agreed with him that less rowdy, more orderly, and more child-friendly celebrations replaced it.

In 1979, the opening of the Halifax Press Club brought light, jokes, romance, political debate, and boozy companionship to The Carleton's spooky old basement. The grey, gritty stones, skillfully jammed together to make one of the walls certainly looked old enough to have been hauled from the wreckage of Louisbourg, and the bar was beautiful. As long as one in an old-time western movie, and made of dark, burnished mahogany, it was where most of us regulars sat side by side to down our drinks and do our opinionating.

I don't remember membership fees or cards, or

anyone's ever being ejected from the "club" for not being one of its members. These included active and retired newspaper reporters and editors, a broadcaster or two, public relations officers and provincial civil servants bored out of their skulls by their jobs, a few freelance writers like me, and just the odd crackpot of one sort or another. On the whole then, it's not surprising that, unlike the Father of the Province and his eminent guests in this very building, the Halifax Press Club has already vanished from the written record. Google it and you'll find nothing, not even a reference to a sports trivia champ.

Yet it was right here that there occurred the battle to determine the Canadian Sports Trivia Champion of 1981. The hometown contender was Harry "The Hat" Flemming. Until expelled from the main men's residence at Mount Allison for repeated offenses fuelled by rum, he and I had been teenage roommates there. During his first days on campus, Harry liked to lure baseball fans among the students into betting against him on, say, the number of strikeouts Boston pitcher Lefty Grove threw in 1936. With the bet in place, he'd yank a baseball record book from a back pocket to prove he was right and the other guy wrong, and collect his winnings. Word spread. Within a week, no one would bet against him on anything.

His marks at Mount A were only so-so but if he'd cared to apply his fabulous memory to his studies, he'd have graduated summa cum laude. His subscription to *Time* magazine was unusual in itself among Mount A students, but his effortlessly filing in his brain just about every fact in every issue was phenomenal. When it came to knowledge for knowledge's sake, the mature

Harry could more than hold his own not only with respect to sports, but in the fields of movies, Italian tenors, country and western music, British and Canadian history, Nova Scotian political history, U.S. presidential politics, German generals of World War II, and the unpronounceable names of cabinet ministers in African nations. Though sports trivia was certainly his vocation, he had a whole string of mere hobbies. He graduated from the Dalhousie Law School but never practised law. Harry was a newspaperman, TV interviewer, radio commentator, magazine columnist, journalism teacher, federal bureaucrat, executive director of the Atlantic Provinces Economic Council, and chief policy adviser to the premier of Nova Scotia. But more satisfying to him than anything he achieved in any of these sidelines was having *The Sporting News* ("The Bible of Baseball") publish his blunt correction of an error in a story by none other than American novelist John Updike about baseball immortal Ted Williams.

By the time Harry's private passion emerged in public performances he was a bald, bespectacled, cigar-puffing, thin-lipped, and habitually scowling gent in his mid-forties. The trivia craze had begun to sweep all across North America. Two journeymen newspaper editors in Montreal marketed a board game they'd invented called *Trivial Pursuit*. Tens of millions of buyers would soon be snapping it up and, in different languages and versions, *Trivial Pursuit* would eventually rack up sales worth more than a billion dollars.

Since Halifax had more bars per capita than most Canadian cities and, for my money, more Saturday night house parties as well, it offered fertile ground for trivia contests. For one about sports that a couple of Harry's cronies designed to increase the business of a struggling bar they favoured, he agreed to compete every Saturday afternoon. He instantly proved not only unbeatable, but obnoxiously unbeatable. His arrogance and smarter-than-thou manner made every opponent hot and desperate to bring him low. If a question put to him struck him as insultingly easy, he responded in the same spirit as President Lyndon Johnson's notorious reply to a query from a Washington reporter: "You're asking me, the leader of the Western world, a chicken-shit question like that?"

With Harry thumping challenger after challenger during 100-question afternoons, and sports nuts crowding in to witness the slaughter, the happy owners of the bar renamed it The Trivia Lounge and, after each contest, rewarded him with $50 (worth triple that in 2020 currency) of free drinking. Since I never saw him lose a sports trivia competition, I have no idea whether he'd have been a good or bad loser but, in victory, he was lordly.

He bought rounds for friends and vanquished alike, and the $50 did not go far. He'd arrive home out of pocket but feeling fine, thank you, and with another trophy to show his wife (whom he married in 1960, the year Pirates infielder Bill Mazeroski clouted his immortal bottom-of-the-ninth home run, and thereby demolished the Yankees in the seventh game of the World Series). Harry won so many dinky cups on pedestals that she finally asked, "Why don't they ever give you something useful, like an ashtray?"

The peak of Harry's career was his duel at The Press Club against a celebrated sports trivia gunslinger from out of town. At fifty-one, Brodie Snyder was not only the author of books about the Montreal Expos and the guy who supplied the trivia question for the Expos TV broadcasts, but a former news editor and sports editor of the Montreal *Gazette*. "When you walked into the newsroom, there he was with his sleeves rolled up yelling instructions," one of his admirers there would remember. "He was the real thing. If they made a movie about the gruff old news editor, it would be him. Black coffee, cigarettes and scotch. He was a legend." The legend included "his uncanny memory for minor details," and domination of barroom arguments about, yes, sports trivia.

Harry had once been very much the same kind of bird. Remembering him as he was in the editorial department of *The Chronicle Herald* way back in the 1960s, the lawyer, journalist, and long-time Liberal insider Brian Flemming wrote, "Harry was straight from central casting for some movie classic like *The Front Page*. The iconic Harry wore his trademark fedora on the back of his head, smoked like an ancient steam-driven train, and drank more than his fair share of single-malt whisky." As for dominating barroom arguments, well, for the better part of half a century there was never any shortage of Halifax whisky drinkers to vouch for that.

Is it nonsense to claim that a national championship could hang on the outcome of just one battle between a guy from Halifax and another from Montreal? Well, maybe, but from Québec out to British Columbia, Canada often seemed either united in contempt for the Maritimes or forgetful of their very existence. For my purposes then, there was no reason why a Montrealer couldn't represent all of the

Canadians up there. Besides, that night the CBC would flash a bit of the contest on *The National*, and surely that alone meant the championship at stake was truly national.

As the show began, Snyder was charming enough in his tough, Montreal-Scottish way, but perhaps a bit cocky. You could scarcely squeeze a sardine into the club, and the crowd included even a few locals who, like those who once prayed for the downfall of Muhammad Ali, yearned to see the humbling of the unhumble Harry the Hat. Snyder, who'd written a couple of books about the Montreal Expos, naturally sported an Expos cap. Never big on Canadian nationalism, Harry wore the cap of the winningest and most arrogant ball team in big-league history, the New York Yankees.

As the lights of the CBC crew glared at the contenders, sweat streamed down their faces. Especially Snyder's. After a dozen questions, he wore the bewildered, panicky look of a third-rate club fighter who realizes in the first round that he has somehow climbed into the ring with a title-bound brute who is about to give him a hideous pummelling. The ensuing rounds were not a pretty sight. When the score reached 52-18 in Harry's favour, Snyder threw in his Expo hat.

After that night, Harry pretty well quit competing and became a sort of grand middle-aged man of the Halifax trivia subculture. He served as the surprisingly amiable emcee for contests in general trivia at The Press Club and, at a north-end tavern, put in a winter of Saturdays as the guy who fired the questions at sports trivia contests for younger men. "Some of the kids who are coming up today are fantastic," he told me. "They can answer questions on fourth-round draft choices, for Chrissakes." He lowered his voice, looked around, and finally confided, "They could probably even take me, you know. But only on the past fifteen years. They actually study for the goddamn contests, but they don't know from shit about the grand sweep of baseball history."

His trivia victories set him firmly on his way to a kind of stardom as Halifax's bluntest, grumpiest, and most outspoken character of the late twentieth and early twenty-first centuries. The ever-more conservative Harry and journalist Parker Donham, a raving socialist by comparison, wrangled about Nova Scotia politics once a week for fifteen years on the CBC's supper-hour news show, *1ˢᵗ Edition*. "Politics is Nova Scotia's favourite spectator sport," Donham wrote in 2000. "Our unruly debates have helped make *1ˢᵗ Edition* the most popular CBC program here, attracting nearly twice as many viewers as *The National*, or *the fifth estate*." If my performance on *Gazette* had been disastrous, Harry's – on *1ˢᵗ Edition*'s "Harry and Parker Show," year after year in the same time slot – was nothing short of triumphant.

As a long-time political columnist for the *Halifax Daily News*, he was fearless, straight-shooting, and, among his more liberal readers, frequently infuriating. His feistiness also popped up in letters to other newspapers and his soundings-off on CBC's *Information Morning*. In the same week in February 2008 that the *Daily News* folded, Harry died at seventy-four. I am lucky to have once known him as a close friend.

If Harry was a memorable denizen of the part of Bulkeley's basement that emerged as The Press Club, so was the mysterious and eccentric American southerner, Pat Murphy. I say mysterious because I never knew why he showed up in Halifax in 1974; how he'd promptly rounded up enough money to found *Axiom*, a bimonthly magazine for Maritimers and Newfoundlanders; or by what magical powers of persuasion he won for me a trip to the finest hotels in Hong Kong, in Kuala Lumpur in Malaysia, in Jakarta and on a sumptuous beach in Bali in Indonesia, in Sydney and Canberra in Australia, and Wellington, New Zealand.

Pat had discovered not only that External Affairs Minister Allan J. MacEachen, the most powerful federal politician ever to come out of Cape Breton, was to make an official sweep through Southeast Asia, but also that he would end his trip with a sentimental visit to Waipu (say "why poo"). That's a village in northern New Zealand. Not even most New Zealanders have heard of it, but its people are nearly all descendants of some eight hundred Presbyterian highlanders whom the Rev. Norman McLeod, a tall, autocratic, and hypnotic preacher, led there in the 1850s from the St. Ann's neighbourhood in Cape Breton.

St. Ann's was in MacEachen's riding, and he had sat in the kitchens of families that still farmed the same land and fished the same waters that the Normanites had left. The story of McLeod and his followers, who built with their own hands all six of the ships for their exodus, and sailed them more than 10,000 miles, remains legendary to descendants of both the voyagers and those who stayed behind.

MacEachen certainly didn't lose any votes in Cape Breton-Highlands-Canso by showing up at Waipu on the other side of the globe, but his motive was more emotional than calculating. He speechified there in Gaelic, and his audience was a rapt crowd of ringers for Cape Breton Islanders. As four beautiful New Zealand children, in brilliant Highland gear and accompanied by skilled pipers, skipped, pranced, and flung their way through a double sword dance and Reel of Tulloch, MacEachen looked as though he thought this was the best show on Earth. You couldn't observe him in Waipu without knowing that, in him, as the old "Canadian Boat Song" puts it, "The blood is strong, the heart is Highland."

So perhaps it didn't really take magical persuasion by Pat Murphy for me to find myself tagging along as the least important journalist on an official tour of Southeast Asia. For his magazine, the least important of the media outlets invited, I would write exclusively about events in the least important of our destinations. In the capitals of five nations, MacEachen met presidents and prime ministers, generals and cabinet ministers, ambassadors and mandarins. He discussed Canada's record as a Pacific power, the billions that the Canadian government and industry had invested in Southeast Asia, the Law of the Sea, postwar Vietnam, Soviet sea power, U.S. sea power, Canada's role in helping Asian nations stand as a bulwark against communism, and a dozen other momentous issues.

Everywhere the tour took us, the thunder of the ideological struggles of the times seemed as ominous to me as the volcanoes, earthquakes, and floods we'd just escaped. The media gang included reporters from major Canadian newspapers and all three national TV networks, as well as their camera crews. These guys had never heard of *Axiom*. They all knew one another

but, except possibly as a writer whose byline occasionally appeared in *Maclean's*, not me. What was I doing
among them?

Was I a spy, gathering evidence for a Canadian
version of Timothy Crouse's best seller, *The Boys on
the Bus*? That book included highly uncomplimentary
revelations about the "pack journalism" of reporters
who covered the 1972 presidential election campaigns
in the U.S, and the national reporter for CTV warned
me, "Bruce, if you're writing a *Boys on the Bus* about us,
I'm going to punch you right in the face."

I assured him that he and the other boys on our
Waipu-bound government jet just weren't interesting
enough for that and, as things turned out, I confined
all my writing about this exotic junket to a 2,800-word
story in *Axiom* that Pat entitled, "Allan J. MacEachen:
At home with New Zealand's 'Bluenosers.'"

I ended it with this: "The pipers send us off
with 'Scotland the Brave,' but just before we leave,
MacEachen mails ten postcards to addresses on Cape
Breton Island. On each card, he writes, five words: 'I
made it to Waipu.'"

If ever there were a Halifax come-from-away who
turned out to be a "character," it was Pat Murphy. When
he assigned me to the Waipu story, he appeared to be
living by little more than his wits but had somehow
found a house on Harbourview Avenue, in the well-
heeled South End, as a home for himself and *Axiom*. I
knew him best as a fellow habitué of The Press Club.
Tall and dishevelled, with a shock of messy white hair,
he was as addicted to talking as he was to booze. His
voice, rich with a North Carolina accent and usually loud, ranged in tone from amiable to outrage. His

best friend, communications and public relations consultant Guy Pothier, remembered him as a free spirit who "reveled in the gratuitous act, despised bad faith in himself and others," and was contemptuous of not only middle-class values but of authority.

This last attitude may have inspired Halifax police to arrest him for public drunkenness a little more often than necessary. As they shoved him into a paddy wagon one night, a constable said, "Got you again, Tex," and he furiously replied, "Ah'm not from Texas, dammit! Ah'm from North Carolina."

Learning from Pothier about Pat's higher education was like discovering that some Spring Garden Road panhandler had once been a surgeon. Pat, it turns out, studied at Yale and Heidelberg universities, wrote his Ph.D. thesis on one of the most important philosophers of the twentieth century, Martin Heidegger, and taught philosophy at American Universities. He knew James Baldwin in New York, and in London once spent a raucous night of hard drinking with Colin Wilson, author of the sensationally bestselling *The Outsider* (1956), and more than a hundred other books.

After two failed marriages in the U.S. in the 1960s, Pat popped up in Prince Edward Island just when its bold experiment in sustainable living, The Ark, was arousing international publicity and attracting to the province scientists, hippies, and counterculture idealists. By 1974, he had settled in Halifax, and apparently felt at home at last. It was here and in nearby East Dover that he spent the rest of his life. He died in 2009.

Late one Friday night in 1979, when The Press Club was full of talky drinkers, who did Penny and I take there as our guest but that supreme shit-disturber,

Mordecai Richler. Of course, he was also exactly what
our mutual friend, critic Robert Fulford, would one
day call him: "The great shining star of his Canadian
literary generation."

While becoming that star, however, he so offended
his fellow Jews in Montreal that many denounced him
as a "Jewish anti-Semite." Later, he enraged Québécois
with his vivid revelations about the anti-Semitism that
had infected so many of the powerful in twentieth-cen-
tury Québec; his sarcastic and bitterly witty attacks on
the separatist movement; and his making the province's
laws to protect the French language from pollution by
English look as ludicrous as men in tutus. Horrors! He
was "not a real Quebecker."

While I'd edited three or four of his articles for
Maclean's in the early '60s and seen him at a cocktail
party in Toronto, we barely knew each other. In 1968,
however, when critics mauled his latest novel, *Cocksure*,
as a smart-alecky exhibition of obscenities, I gave it a
full page of praise in *The Star Weekly*, which came out
every week all over the country. If not a close friend
then, I was a kindred spirit, and *Cocksure* turned out to
be a Governor General's Award winner.

On one of his rare visits to Halifax in the late '70s,
someone took him to a Christmas party at the provincial legislature where, as he told me, various members
of Premier Regan's cabinet "had their tongues down
their secretaries' throats." He also made a memorable appearance on Peter Gzowski's unmemorable talk
show. When Peter mentioned pop singer Anne Murray,
Mordecai asked, "Who's Anne Murray?" I still believe
he'd never heard of her, but the studio audience saw
him as a detestable smart-arse from central Canada

who'd deliberately insulted the pride of Springhill, and tried to boo him right out of the building.

It was because Mordecai loved press clubs that we took him to Halifax's but, looking back, I realize he had no idea just how weird this one could be on a busy night. We hadn't been seated at the bar more than ten minutes when one of its familiar loonies marched up to him to shout, "There are no Jews in Guysborough County, Richler." Mordecai said, "That's interesting," and the dork, looking baffled, quietly retreated. Meanwhile, in an armchair to one side of us sat a civil servant who was habitually surly when sober, but was now seething with hostility. "Bruce," he finally blurted, "you're nothing but Risshlerg's goddamned flack, and you're getting paid to show the bastard around."

To explain that he and I were friends, Mordecai sat down in the armchair opposite him, but that inspired the sorehead to announce, "I'm a Jesuit-trained hishtorian, Risshlerg, and I say to you the so-called holocaust is a complete and utter fabrication. The Nazis did not kill six million Jews during World War Two."

Welcome to Nova Scotia, Mordecai.

I was shaking with rage, but he seemed to find this creep amusing.

"Okay then," he said. "Let's say they just killed five and a half million."

"Nobody proved that. Nobody, but nobody, knew that."

"They knew," Mordecai replied.

He was calm, and as tough as a catcher's mitt. A little while later, Penny went to the club's foyer to get some lipstick from her coat, and there was Mordecai, alone and scribbling in a notepad. One day, I thought, the Jesuit-trained holocaust-denier might just find himself in a bestselling novel.

He was staying at our house, and at seven the next morning, early for me, I went downstairs to find him seated at the kitchen table, and deep in conversation with our ten-year-old son, Max. They were talking as though they'd long been the best of friends. Mordecai may well have been the most cutting, sarcastic, and combative writer in the history of Canadian letters, but while chatting with our curly-haired little boy on that long-gone morning he had the kindest expression I have ever seen on a man's face.

9

Halifax Kept Coming Back Like a Song

If in early June, 1984, Halifax were an old car with a manual transmission, the arrival of the world's most magnificent tall ships beside our great new harbour-front boardwalk shifted the whole drab town into a superhigh gear it had never known before. The ships came from thirteen nations, no fewer than fifty-eight topsail schooners, brigs, brigantines, barques, barquentines, and towering square-riggers. None anchored out in the harbour, as they'd had to do in port after port on both sides of the Atlantic, because they could now tie up, every last one of them, bow to stern, beside that long, beamy, generous boardwalk.

For six freakishly hot, sunny days, hundreds of young crewmen, strikingly handsome in their home-lands' naval uniforms, mingled with tens of thousands of us happy Haligonians, and tourists from foreign ports and throughout Canada. Busloads of girls from the Bluenose boonies arrived to date the foreign sailors, and the mingled smells of perfume, suntan oil, hot-dogs, beer, expectation, and romance floated up and down the boardwalk. It all added up to one long, joyous international festival. Nowhere else in the world was there a better place for it.

Too soon, crowds gathered on rooftops and water-fronts to clap and whoop farewells as each vessel sailed down the harbour, out past Point Pleasant Park, and off to Québec City and Europe. That was the happiest of the more than six hundred weeks since I'd settled here, and I still remember the arrival of the boardwalk, which welcomed all those ships, as a marvellous harbinger of a better Halifax to come. If no cappuccino place had opened its doors here in the 1970s, and if not one restaurant had dared serve a meal under a sun umbrella on the sidewalk, neither had any cruise ship or international festival sailed into town.

Ahh, but the '80s. They brought us not only that Parade of Sail, but the Atlantic Film Festival (1981), the International Buskers Festival (1986), Atlantic Jazz Festival (1987), and the Pride March for gays and lesbians (1988). While that first Pride parade was limited to a couple of streets in the north end, and only seventy-five brave souls took part – for fear of being identified, some pulled paper bags over their heads – nearly three thousand now get together on a summer Saturday every year and, before as many as 100,000 cheering spectators, walk, strut, dance, and joyously flag-wave their way through the very heart of the city.

The festivals seemed to have emerged from a kind of subconscious recognition among Haligonians that it was time to awaken and celebrate the little port's culture and cosmopolitanism. Halifax could be a city. By the early '90s, daMaurizio at the Old Brewery Market on Lower Water Street and Bish on the harbourfront boardwalk both offered superb dining influenced by culinary traditions of northern Italy. Old Man Moriah's, with gourmet cookery from Greece, had sprung up on southern Barrington Street. For fine seafood downtown, McKelvie's now competed with The Five Fishermen and, if Craig Claiborne had only returned to Halifax, he'd have been delighted by the décor, linen, silverware, service, and cooking in the intimate dining room at the Haliburton House Inn on Morris Street.

Then there was La Cave. To reach it, you had to walk through a little tunnel between shops on the south side of Blowers Street. Its ersatz air of secrecy and, more important, the delicious dinners it served until after two a.m. made it popular among younger carousers. Night life was booming beyond midnight. Loyal Haligonian John DeMont reported in *Maclean's* that Halifax had started to hum with energy and to become "a boisterous good-time city of the moment." In 1893, Rudyard Kipling had solemnly called it "The Warden of the Honour of the North," but exactly a century later, Manhattan-based fashion magazine *Harper's Bazaar* decided it was something far more important: "the very anatomy of a hip city." Other magazines in Britain and the U.S. touted its "exploding music scene." Owing to the grungy style of its indie rock bands, Halifax had even become "the next Seattle."

In 1995, a show that would have been unimaginable in the Halifax I knew in the '70s occurred in a renovated warehouse down by the boardwalk.

American poet Allen Ginsberg, the controversial, widely reviled, and proudly homosexual "voice of the next generation," performed alongside Ashley MacIsaac, the sensational young Celtic fiddler from Cape Breton, whose repulsive onstage antics would soon make him more famous even than his phenomenal playing.

Their weird gig was a tribute to Rangdrol Mukpo, who had just succeeded his deceased father, Chogyam Trungpa, as head of the worldwide Shambhala Bhuddist network. Two decades before, Trungpa had inexplicably transferred the headquarters of Shambahla International from Colorado to Halifax, and hundreds of the movement's adherents, most of them well-educated Americans, followed him to form the world's largest community of non-Asian Buddhists. Not since the British first arrived in 1749 had such a big batch of come-from-aways showed up in Halifax.

If Ginsberg-MacIsaac aroused the amusement of locals, the G-7 economic summit, only a month later, aroused the attention of the entire world. Meeting every year in a different city, the summit enabled the leaders of the seven nations with the most advanced economies to discuss face to face the economic, political, and other crises that threaten global security. For this one, wrote Stephen Kimber, one of the city's most skilled reporters, "Halifax hosted a massive, continuous downtown street party for residents and visitors, including thousands of international government officials and media."

We missed that street party. In the late '80s and most of the '90s, we missed just about everything that sprang from the improving Halifax. We just weren't here. We had never really been anywhere for long.

For sixteen years after our marriage in 1955, Penny and I lived not in Halifax, but consecutively at two addresses in Ottawa, two in London, England, another in Ottawa, and then one in Toronto, one in Santa Monica, California, three more in Toronto – where our children were born in the '60s – a house in Newcastle, Ontario, yet another in Ottawa, and, finally, the Newcastle place again. Albert Einstein said, "Life is like riding a bicycle. To keep your balance, you must keep moving." But when we quit Ontario for Nova Scotia, we were in our mid-thirties and dreamed of keeping our balance not on bicycles but in the house we'd love for the rest of our lives. We never found it.

Within two years of my having settled our family out near Prospect in that colony of disillusioned come-from-aways, Penny found a fine wooden, three-storey house for sale on York Street in the heart of the city. We snapped it up, lived in it with our children for eight years, a long time for us, and then sold it to buy a duplex just across LeMarchant Street from Dalhousie's Killam Memorial Library. After that, we bought, occupied, and sold condos on Lilac Street and Artillery Place and, in partnership with our daughter Annabel – who brought into our late lives the miracle of her infant son, Gabriel – duplexes on Willow Street, Quinpool Road, and, finally, Second Street.

The place on Willow, just one boarding house west of Robie, was more than a century old, and so loaded with antique charm that we fell for it despite our real estate agent's gently suggesting, "This is not really a family neighbourhood." After our new weed-eater vanished from our backyard in broad daylight, a hysterical and dishevelled woman pounded on our front

144 – Halifax and Me

door while fleeing a man who'd been beating her, the lower flat in the duplex beside ours turned into a brothel, and drunken teenagers decided our driveway was a good place to piss, we decided that perhaps our agent had a point. Nor did it make our dwelling any more family-friendly that during the morning rush hour that surrounded us on North, Robie, and Willow streets the traffic was so heavy that the window panes in Penny's and my bedroom shuddered in time with throbbing automobile engines. The air pollution must have rivalled industrial China's.

Once our children were out on their own, and we'd bought and sold this absurd variety of dwellings nicely inside Halifax, we rode Einstein's bike to an absurd number of dwellings farther and farther away from Halifax. First, Penny and I bought from my aunt Bess the old Bruce homestead on Highway 344 in Guysborough County, and after she died in 1986, moved in forever. That was the idea anyway. I would do what my father had dreamed of doing but died in Toronto before he could even try: live year-round as a full-time writer at the farmhouse in Port Shoreham where he was born.

In the middle of our curving field to the south stood a tough, shapely little apple tree that some years sprouted a few apple blossoms and other years didn't. Beyond that rose a wall of spruce and firs and, in the distance, the great blue sweep of Chedabucto Bay. Above the far shore stretched a purplish blur of hills. At night we could see the blink-blink-blink of the Queensport Light over there, and the waterfront lights of nine or so houses and cottages.

With the black flies gone, the barn swallows still

chittering, the sunshine strong all day, and the bay marching before a brisk southwesterly, the homestead often seemed a daily paradise. Near the little apple tree we flew our kite under a double rainbow. We never tired of the gull-haunted beach. Scores of times, we started from our own stretch of sandy shore and walked for miles beside gentle or crashing breakers all the way out to Ragged Head and back. On rare nights when the bay was almost warm, and even on some when it felt as icy as the Greenland Sea, we tumbled and flopped around in it naked. Yow! Talk about refreshing! A couple of slugs of rum beside a crackling bonfire completed the exercise.

Outside the old house a little way inland, we stood among fireflies some nights, and marvelled at the storms of uncountable stars that sparkled from horizon to horizon. Morning or afternoon, it was satisfying just to gaze out a front window, first installed by Richard Harvey Bruce about 140 years earlier, to contemplate our weather-beaten workshop and woodshed. They looked so right.

That whole house always looked right. After 1953, it had running water, electricity, and an oil-heated furnace, but we installed in the kitchen a new and, for its time, super-efficient wood-burning range. With split and well-dried maple, plus a little know-how, we could heat the whole place with that range, even the four upstairs bedrooms. But they didn't need much heat. They were the tiniest bedrooms any of us ever slept in, with ceilings so low the early Bruces in these parts must have been extremely short. We crammed one downstairs room with all our books, and all the jazz, rock, folk, and classical music we had on vinyl records, CDs, and cassette tapes. With big speakers, a turntable, and Sony tuner (now a quarter-century old and still working), we could play it all. Music always sounded better there than anywhere else.

Over three and a half decades in the late 1900s and these early 2000s, two of our three children and our grandchildren have joined us at the house for Thanksgiving dinners and birthday parties. Our great-grandchildren, too, have begun to get a taste of the place. There has scarcely ever been a summer that Penny and I, as well as some of them, haven't escaped to the homestead for a weekend or longer. More than any other dwelling we've ever known, it is "home." We raised our children in one Halifax house for eight full years and in another lived out our entire seventies. We spent thousands upon thousands more days and nights in the houses we bought in Halifax than we ever did at the homestead in Port Shoreham, yet once inside that creaking old place for even an hour we invariably agreed that, yes, this was our only real home.

And so it was – for four years.

Winter crept up on me. It sometimes laid down a sheet of ice so hard and slippery it left every vehicle paralyzed in a barn or garage, imprisoned all humans in their houses, and, were it not for Penny, would have turned me into a raving victim of solitary confinement. When the temperature rose enough to allow blizzards to brew and me to venture nine miles into Guysborough, what drove me back into semi-solitary confinement at the homestead were the dreadful sights and sounds of winter in the boondocks: spinning tires, charging snowplows, branches cracking off trees, snowmobiles *braaaaping* in distant woods, impotent car engines going *ruh, ruh, ruh,* and, at the grocery store, some lamebrains sneezing on fruit and vegetables, others coughing like erupting volcanoes in every aisle, and still others chirping, "Cold enough for ya?" Could I not go for a walk till my spirits recovered? What a sick joke. I had no snowshoes. I had to plod along the shoulders of Highway 344. Cars with their nighttime headlights on, a dismal sight at noon, splashed salt-laden slush on my pants. The whole countryside, covered with snow beneath a sky the colour of my father's gravestone, was stupendously boring.

In the heart of Halifax, a blizzard was a nuisance, but it didn't sink you in unshakeable gloom. It was something bank tellers and liquor-store cashiers joked about with their customers, but it didn't make you want to lie down and beat the floor with your fists. Indeed, it gave Haligonians a bit of that we're-all-in-this-together feeling that Londoners knew during World War II.

In the country, winter imprisoned you. Halifax set you free. You didn't have to take your walk on a lonely highway here. You could amble along beside the slopes of a downtown park where tobogganing youngsters screamed out their happiness, join window shoppers in a heated mall, poke around at a crafts fair, explore the Art Gallery or the Maritime Museum, take in the blues at Bearly's, or dine at Ryan Duffy's. It offered not only the best steaks in Halifax but, since it was upstairs on Spring Garden Road and overlooked the city's busiest intersection, the best people-watching as well.

We are people-watchers, not bird-watchers. The closest people to us in Port Shoreham were the Mac-Intoshes. They had farmed the property next to ours in the west for generations, and we could not possibly have had more friendly, helpful, generous, or entertaining neighbours. But merely to say good morning face to face with any of them, we had to go up our long steep driveway to Highway 344, and then west on 344 for the length of a football field to their letterbox, and south on their driveway for another football field to their house. In Halifax, I could say, "Good morning" to neighbours over a backyard fence, or while getting *The Chronicle Herald* from our front porch, or as I walked to our car, which was parked by our side door, and itching to whiz me downtown to people worth watching in the good old wintertime.

On more and more Friday mornings during the winters of the late '80s at Port Shoreham, I asked Penny, "Hey, why don't we slip into Halifax for a day or two?" And a few hours later, coming down the Trans-Canada Highway, "Where'll we go for dinner tonight?"

"Oh, I don't know. Let's decide when we get to the hotel."

As we crossed the old bridge and headed south on Barrington, darkness was beginning to settle on all the steeples and towers. A pink blush faded from the sky over Citadel Hill, and the lights of tens of thousands of neighbours were beginning to twinkle all across the little city by the sea.

Remembering those dashes to Halifax, I also remember Canadian novelist Hugh Hood's "You can take the boy out of the city, but you can't take the city out of the boy." I once dismissed this as too glib by half, but came to see it as a truth of the ages. And why wouldn't it be true of me? By 1987, when I vowed to spend the rest of my life in Port Shoreham, hadn't I lived virtually every one of my fifty-three years in Toronto, Ottawa, London, or Halifax? I may have shovelled a lot of manure in my time, but none of the real kind on a farm.

In the winter of 1991, when the Atlantic Salmon Federation (ASF) offered me interesting money to do interesting work some 375 miles west of the Bruce homestead, I finally accepted that, although our old house was "home," that could not mean in winter. The international headquarters of ASF, which was dedicated to the well-being of wild Atlantic salmon and supported by, among others, stinking-rich anglers from the U.S. and Canada, was just outside St. Andrews, New Brunswick. That's where I now went to edit ASF's slick quarterly, *The Atlantic Salmon Journal*.

No, it was not a city, but about 1,600 people lived there year-round, and its natural charms made it popular for tourists and lovable for the "summer people" who owned wooden mansions there. Generations ago tourism boosters had given the town a cutesy nickname that still sticks: St. Andrews By-the-Sea. Protected by islands at the head of Passamaquoddy Bay, the pretty little port of St. Andrews lies hard by the mouth of the St. Croix River, which is the border between Canada and the U.S.

Since our house was practically next door to the mighty Algonquin Resort, streams of happy tourists, chattering in a dozen languages, passed our front door while walking down to Water Street. That's the main drag for whale-watching boats, waterfront pubs, arts and craft shops, lobster rolls, and guides to historic sites, architectural treasures, and remarkable horticultural gardens. For more than a century the Algonquin has catered to well-heeled visitors who crave to get their bodies pampered, or to play golf on a superior bayside course, or just to inhale the salty ocean air, which stupendous tides made especially fragrant.

The only drawback to summertime life in St. Andrews for us was that on weekends we had to jam our cheap little power mower into the trunk of our car, hurtle off to Port Shoreham, race with the mower all over the grassy, bumpy, soggy "lawn" that surrounded the venerable house there, then grab a night's sleep, and hurtle back to St. Andrews – not forgetting the mower because the lawn there also had to be mowed, and that took another three hours. The trip to and from Port Shoreham, including the mowing and two meals on the road, took fourteen hours. Then in October, at St. Andrews, we had to rake up enough dead maple leaves to fill thirty big brown paper bags.

In time, what we loved most about St. Andrews was its proximity to Saint John. While driving from Port Shoreham to Halifax took three hours, we could hop from St. Andrews into Saint John in just one. With only about 75,000 people, it was a puny city to be sure, but those people were intensely loyal to their town and, among the natives of all the cities I've ever visited, these were the most helpful to strangers I've ever known. I had only to open a street map on lower King Street to have a true-blue Saint Johner stop to ask if I wanted directions, or offer to walk along with me until we reached my destination.

In a fit of braggadocio back in the '80s, Saint John concocted as its official nickname The Greatest Little City in the East. This, of course, is nonsense. Halifax was and remains the greatest little city in the east. Saint

John, however, did have certain enduring charms beyond the friendliness of its people. In the old business district we loved to explore a couple of dusty junk and antique stores (gone now); eat at a little restaurant whose food was as good as its name was imaginative, Incredible Edibles; and just walk beside elegant old row housing that had that Boston "brownstone" look.

And we never skipped the City Market. Dating back a couple of centuries, the oldest continuously operating market in Canada, it sloped down a full city block. Inside, it was a carnival of fresh, fresh food under a mighty arc of old, old history. Look right there! Laid out on ice, it's haddock, scallops, cod, and sole, right out of the ocean. And over there! Red peppers, green onions, yellow potatoes, purple eggplants, and a dozen other veggies, pulled from rich earth only this morning. Now, look straight up! Surely you're standing under the upturned hull of a mighty clipper ship that will soon circle the globe.

At ASF headquarters, I had a big corner office in one of two little buildings where I worked not in the usual loneliness of the freelance writer but among thirty men and women, most of whom thought I was some sort of bigshot. To get there, I usually rode my bicycle along a scenic waterfront path for all of three miles. Since ASF never objected to anything that appeared in their magazine under my editorship, I felt I didn't really have a boss. Yet my pay was good and absolutely reliable, and I was free to sell anything I wanted to other publications. By 1995, after four years with ASF, I knew that no freelancer could ask for anything more.

So in 1996 we fled St. Andrews and set up camp in a furnished apartment in the heart of Montreal. Why?

Well, on November 17, 1995, in the biggest and most astounding financial transaction in Canadian history up to that time, 83,800,000 shares of the government-owned CN fetched $2.16 billion and, in the months since, this newly privatized CN had already proved itself ever-more efficient and ever-more profitable. CN, with its headquarters in Montreal, wanted me to write a book about the tactics, machinations, and steely determination that lay behind the transformation of this "state-owned monster" into a stock-market darling.

The story was more exciting than the landing of any monster salmon in the Restigouche would ever be, and the bait that CN dangled before me was irresistible: a good monthly income, an office of my own at CN headquarters, use of the CN library, interviews with top CN executives; all-expenses-paid trips with Penny to Toronto and New York, where I would interview the investment bankers who'd played such dramatic roles in the privatization; and, finally, that fully furnished, two-bedroom apartment in the thirty-three-storey Plaza Tower, which was above a heated swimming pool, a shopping mall that smelled like a thousand freshly baked croissants every morning, and the Atwater Subway Station.

CN was calling, "All Abooooaaard!"

Off we went.

Au revoir, notre cher Halifax.

10

Hurricane Juan, and Blundering Off to Vancouver

My book for CN, entitled *The Pig that Flew: The Battle to Privatize Canadian National,* was published in the fall of '97, earned enough applause to please both me and the railroad's brass, and freed us to return to the old plan of settling for the rest of our lives at the Bruce homestead. But as early as January of '98 we suffered such a dismal bout of cabin fever there that we booked two big adjoining rooms in a corner of the Lord Nelson Hotel for all of February.

And then? Second thoughts. The fridge in this suite was tiny, cooking was forbidden, and, on the day we looked the rooms over, they felt cold enough for hanging carcasses of beef. We cancelled the reservation, and made a fat down payment on a top-floor, two-bedroom condo only a block away. It had a skylight above a neat, galley kitchen, and one of its two bathtubs was big enough for basketball ace Michael

Jordan to splash around in comfortably. The view from the balcony, living room, and both bedrooms looked southward over Spring Garden Road, and all the way out to the open horizon of the Atlantic Ocean. No second thoughts here. Penny estimated I was deeply in love with this condo twelve seconds after seeing it.

We could see a bit of the harbour from the balcony, and while standing out there one October evening when I was sixty-six I glimpsed the last cruise ship of the season as it left port. In my eyes cruise ships were still a novelty. We had never seen even one in our earliest years here and during the later growth of the business in Halifax, we'd mostly been somewhere else. Some two decades later, nearly two hundred cruise ships would visit between late April and early November every year. They'll spill more than 300,000 visitors from scores of nations onto the boardwalk and nearby streets. Heaven knows how many of these rubberneckers tell their friends later about this beautiful, historic, and fascinating little city.

But back to my vision from the balcony. All the lights on four decks of the ship gleamed through heavy mist. I imagined hundreds of couples dressing for dinner. Moving in a stately way, the vessel disappeared behind a skyscraper, but her big, beamy stern reappeared off Point Pleasant Park. Then the fog swallowed her whole. In a couple of days, I was sure, she'd be passing the Statue of Liberty on her way up to Manhattan. Every now and then Halifax makes me idiotically romantic and, as that ship slipped away in the distance, I was once again eighteen.

On January 2, 2002, Annabel gave birth to Gabriel in Vancouver and three months later brought him home to Halifax. She wanted him to grow up within a loving family. He certainly found a loving grandfather. He was ten months old when I told readers of *The Chronicle Herald*, "He is easily the most beautiful baby in the world. Indeed, he is impossibly beautiful. During shopping excursions, I occasionally let my eyes wander from Gabriel to other infants of roughly his age. By comparison, they are at best ordinary, and at worst homely ... I am 68. I have not shared a dwelling with a baby since well before Pierre Elliot Trudeau became a father. Yet Gabriel Bruce has turned me into a man who crawls around on his hands and knees, shouting, 'Come on, Gabey, let's go'; babbles baby-talk in a squeaky voice; and dreams that, at the age of 100, he'll sail catamarans on Chedabucto Bay with a 32-year-old athlete he still knows as 'Good Guy Gabe.'"

For much of Gabriel's first year, we lived with him and Annabel in a rangy old apartment in a Victorian mansion in downtown Saint John. It had once been the city's German consulate, and felt comfortably Victorian. I was under contract to do some writing for J.D. Irving Ltd. One of Canada's mightiest family-owned industrial empires, its corporate headquarters was nearby. As the Irving work expanded, Penny and I sold our Halifax condo with the unforgettable view and bought a cute but roomy house near Joncs Lake in Moncton. Annabel and Gabriel also settled in Moncton, where she went to work in communications for Medavie Blue Cross. Our son Alec, his wife Vivien, and their two daughters had already been Monctonians for seven years. He was among the most skillful freelance writers in Atlantic Canada.

We enjoyed having so much of the family in one

small city, and also the easygoing friendliness of just about every Monctonian we ran into. Still, we could not quite abandon Halifax. It was only 162 miles away by car. Milder than Moncton in winter, cooler and shadier in summer, it had far fewer mosquitos, far more movie screens, a dozen more fine restaurants, a bit of jazz, a bit of blues, a symphony orchestra, and, for us and our children, countless memories.

Besides all that, the Atlantic Ocean, which gave Halifax its harbour, was bigger and better than the Petitcodiac River, which slithered up and down between Moncton and Riverview. Thus it was that on the last weekend in September 2003, Penny and I nipped into Halifax from Moncton for a couple of days, just as we'd nipped into Halifax from Port Shoreham on so many weekends in the late '80s. Only this time, Annabel and her Wonder Boy, Gabriel, were with us. In one car the four of us happily headed straight into the 100-mph fury, with its 145-mph gusts, of the most monstrous storm to smash Halifax in more than a century. How's that for travel planning?

Hurricane Juan tore into tens of thousands of trees in Halifax, felled beloved old giants throughout Point Pleasant Park, inside the Public Gardens, and on streets throughout the city's peninsula. It whipped up sixty-five-foot waves just off Halifax Harbour, knocked out power for nearly 900,000 people, and killed eight people. To witness this heavyweight champion of dirty weather beating up poor old Halifax, and even to feel a bit of the beating, I could scarcely have reserved for us a better located suite. Right downtown on Hollis Street, up on the eighth floor of the Radisson apartment hotel, it had a fine view of all the dark, shifty havoc in the harbour.

In the first roaring minutes of Monday, September 29, Juan walloped Halifax with enough blows to knock it stone cold. Blind in the inky corridor outside our door, Penny felt her way along a wall in a futile search for elevators. Returning to our suite, she plucked an old penlight from her purse, returned to the corridor, and found the elevators. They were dead. Like everything else in the building that required energy, including me, they were useless.

Meanwhile, Annabel was rescuing Gabe. Not yet two years old, he had fallen off the bed they shared and landed in a big puddle. And what created this pond on the carpet of an eighth-floor luxury apartment in a modern hotel? Had the wind been so strong it pushed enough rainwater through window sashes to do the job? Whatever the cause, there was Gabe – alone in deepest darkness, thrashing around in cold water, with nightmarish winds blasting buckets of rain at the window beside his head – and crying. Annabel restored his peace of mind.

From somewhere outside came just enough light for us to make out the tops of a sunken schooner's mast jutting out of the water. Seven-foot-high storm surges, the highest ever seen in the harbour, blasted apart pieces of the boardwalk. Juan picked up erosion-control boulders as big as garbage cans and hurled them onto waterfront parking lots, yet a handful of giddy youths stood out there on that boardwalk with their arms raised on high, and joyfully yelped and bellowed into the face of the storm. They were probably drunk.

They were like the tourists at Peggy's Cove who failed to savour the sea from a distance. Their parents and police would have been aghast to know about their stunt, but I'm sure their own memories of that night will please them all their lives. There's something glorious about a big wind.

By breakfast time, Halifax was a horror to see. The falling of so many great trees had left skies too naked and the light throughout the city oddly raw. As we drove around, looking for a restaurant, any restaurant, that had breakfasts to sell, the sheer brutality of the mugging Juan had inflicted on Halifax sank in on us. Huge old trees had crashed to the ground on street after street. Huge old trunks pinned down parked cars. Huge old networks of roots, torn up from Mother Earth and into the light where they were never meant to be seen, sat exposed, clumpy, and obscene all over the peninsula. They were now the world's ugliest street furniture. Juan had snapped heavy branches off trees, and sent them careering and cartwheeling every which way. Scores of residential streets were thus impassable by car. Live electricity wires thrashed around in the wind.

Here and there people wandered about in the mess. They looked stunned and dazed by the slaughter and maiming of trees so familiar they'd seemed eternal. Did trees have souls? Who knew? But women wept among these felled and broken beings, and I shared their sorrow. I never loved Halifax more. That's why our move to Vancouver only three years later still strikes me as mystifying and lame-brained.

It was in September of 2006, when I was seventy-two and Penny seventy, that we moved with all our furniture almost as far away from Halifax as we could go in Canada. Just moving from one safe address to another inside my homeland – a journey that required no passport, inoculations, Swiss Army knife, or firearm – gave me the tiniest whiff of the satisfaction an ace journalist might feel while secretly sending to *The New York Times* scoops on a revolution in some ruthless dictatorship. I, too, liked doing my work in different places, but ones that weren't all that different. Since I also liked money, the contracts had to be right, too. St. Andrews, Montreal, Saint John, and Moncton all filled the bill, and none were beyond the magnetic power of Halifax. Vancouver was different. It was a crashing mistake. Planning to settle in Vancouver for the rest of our lives, we hired a moving company to take all our furniture out there. We returned to Halifax within eight months. So did all that furniture.

What lay behind this late, brief, and peculiar betrayal of dear old Halifax?

Born in Vancouver, my mother loved it all her life more than she ever loved Toronto and insisted her ashes be interred at its only graveyard. When I was sixteen and crazy about sailing, an old friend of hers brought her nineteen-year-old son to our house from Vancouver and, with a voice like a fledgling CBC announcer's, he bragged about the year-round sailing he did off his hometown. Scheduled racing, by dozens of sloops, throughout the entire Canadian winter … that was an image I couldn't shake for decades.

When I was twenty-three and had worked as a reporter at the *Ottawa Journal* for less than three years, it paid me a supreme compliment. It appointed me to the Parliamentary Press Gallery. I was the Gallery's youngest member. The others included the cream of political reporters from all across Canada. Many, like the two from the *Journal*, were twice my age. The *Journal*'s naming me to join them in the Gallery meant it had its eye on me as a future editor-in-chief, and expected me meanwhile to shine as a political reporter.

I failed to exploit this rare opportunity partly because I was too lazy to do the digging essential to shining, partly because my older partners in the Gallery assigned me nothing but the most trivial stories, and partly because I spent so many hours in a parliamentary reading room poring over the latest editions of the *Vancouver Province*, *Vancouver Sun*, and even the *Prince Rupert Daily News*. After several months, I selected clippings of the best stories of mine the *Journal* had published and sent them off to the managing editor of the *Province* as proof that I was such a hotshot reporter he'd be stupid not to hire me. He never replied, nor even returned my treasured clippings, the thoughtless prick. (Since office photocopiers had yet to be invented, I now had nothing to show other newspapers I might want to work for.) I gave up on the West Coast, waited a year, and joined *The Globe and Mail* in Toronto.

For a couple of weeks when Penny was only twelve, she babysat the infant daughter of her older sister Wendy and her husband, at their home in Santa Monica. Penny would always remember not only the smells of heat, sand, surf, and blossoms beside the Pacific, but a wonderful sense of freedom that floated in the air out there. Her love of southern California even survived our moving there with such high hopes in 1960 but returning to Toronto in such low spirits only seven weeks later. Forty years passed before we next visited Los Angeles, and this time it was to see

Max, our youngest, who lived in West Hollywood. He was thirty-two, a computer animator at Sony Pictures, owner of a black Mustang convertible, and lover of L.A. He'd lived there for four years, and could not imagine anywhere he'd rather spend the rest of his life. Meanwhile, our daughter Annabel, six years older than Max and a whiz at public relations and communications, had also abandoned Halifax for work on the West Coast. She lived in the heart of Vancouver. By then, Wendy and her husband, Vincent Blockley, along with the oldest of their four daughters, Michele – the one Penny had cared for back in the prehistoric times of 1948 – and her husband, Mark Schrader, had long been settled among the rivers and rolling hills at Stanwood in Washington State. Led by Wendy, the family founded and ran a horse farm and riding school there. The drive from Annabel's apartment took little more than two hours.

From time to time during the dozen years that straddled 2000, we visited the West Coast to see Wendy and her family in Stanwood, Max in L.A., and Annabel in Vancouver. After a while, the real Vancouver got me thinking that maybe my ancient fantasies about settling here weren't all that crazy, after all.

Vancouver was a great port beside a great ocean, a great city of nearly 600,000 people that declared its internationalism everywhere you looked. It boasted Stanley Park, which my mother always insisted was the biggest and finest city park in the world, and, best of all, winters so warm snow was a curiosity. Penny, too, liked Vancouver. Climate? Well, it was no L.A., but then it was no Halifax either. Something about its domestic architecture and street design made it feel vaguely Californian. Or maybe it was just having an ocean lying out to the west for a change, or glimpsing people lingering over coffee treats, outdoors in February, while wearing only T-shirts, shorts, and sandals.

So off we went to Vancouver: Penny and me; Gabriel, four years old and back in his birthplace; and Annabel, who still had a high reputation for her work in communications in the British Columbia healthcare industry. She discovered the house we rented on a green and easy stretch of West 16th Avenue. It had two big living rooms, two big bedrooms and one small one, three bathrooms, and a kitchen. We were close to both seductive shopping on south Granville Street and, in the Shaughnessy neighbourhood, the priciest mansions in the city. False Creek and Granville Island were only a few blocks north. The island boasted the most fabulous Public Market and Food Fair I've ever seen, and it was open, and busy, seven days a week.

At first, everything was the way it was supposed to be, the lush greenery soothing, the tiny open ferries on False Creek charming, the explorations on foot everywhere fascinating, the choice of superb restaurants titillating, and the nine city beaches inviting and furnished with the thickest logs in Canada. Day after day after day, the sun shone down benignly on everything from the open ocean to the unchanging mountains. From our neighbourhood, downtown Vancouver looked spiky with its countless skinny skyscrapers. Their backdrop was the jagged row of snowy peaks to the north, and the whole scene told me I was at last alive and kicking in the nirvana of Canada. That feeling lasted maybe one month.

Welcoming broadcasters to a national convention in Vancouver, the Lieutenant Governor of British Columbia, Iona Campagnolo, jokingly described the people of B.C. as "ever the laid-back lotus-eaters of Confederation – always guaranteed to be asleep whenever phoned from distant parts of Canada at five a.m. 'our time' – famed for four-hour lunches and polarized politics." She called this image a "short-hand mythology about B.C.," but before moving to Vancouver in September 2006, I actually believed most of it. In Tennyson's poem, "the mild-eyed melancholy lotus-eaters" fed blossoms from "that enchanted stem" to two of Ulysses' crew. The sailors immediately saw this strange new land as so heavenly that he had to have them dragged back aboard ship and, from everything I'd heard about Vancouver, it, too, was so heavenly its people wanted only to stay there forever.

Whatever narcotic the lotus plant produced, it was marijuana that mightily contributed to the notion that Vancouver was supremely laid-back. So, however, did the kind weather and gorgeous scenery, which supposedly encouraged its people never to let mere work crush them with anxiety or dominate their lives. Wasn't Vancouver bursting with happy hikers, joggers, skiers, kayakers, golfers, rock-climbers, mountain bikers, and lovers of tennis, soccer, fly-fishing, kite-flying, yachting, and fireworks? For hours on sunny, mid-week afternoons, didn't hordes of half-naked (and some fully naked) white-collar workers stretch out on the beaches of English Bay and, using cell phones, pretend they were hard at work in their offices?

Laid-back, right?

Nope.

Vancouver was about as laid-back as Extreme Cage Fighting.

Drivers there jumped lanes with insane recklessness, roared through red traffic lights and crosswalks, passed on the right as though competing in stock-car races, hurtled so close to sidewalks that the smarter pedestrians stayed well back from curbs, and either rocketed across bridges at twice the speed limit or, spewing exhaust fumes, inched over them for hours on end. Seemingly endless rush hours produced a cacophonous symphony of thundering trucks, blaring horns, screeching tires, and bellowed curses. The most common salute among Vancouver drivers was the upraised middle finger.

"At times, Vancouver's a drug-infested hell-hole where people seem so racist, angry and uncivil to each other," an ex-Vancouverite told readers of an Alberta blog. "They get so bloody angry and violent at times ... Not a day goes by without hearing someone screaming in the streets at the top of their lungs." Another ex-Vancouverite, Brian Fawcett, reported on a website that he was guiding a blind friend along a crowded sidewalk when "I heard an angry voice telling us to 'get the (expletive deleted) out of my way,' and found myself eyeball to eyeball with a man about 30 who clearly understood that he'd directed his impatience toward a blind person – and didn't care."

In laid-back Vancouver, I saw hulking men bawl out cowering supermarket cashiers and, in parking lots, rich old ladies, seated in leather behind the steering wheels of BMWs and Mercedes Benzes, furiously snarl at the drivers of lesser vehicles to get the so-and-so out of their way. In the previous year, Vancouverites had assaulted bus drivers more than two hundred times; they cursed, punched, and knifed them, and spat in their faces. Vancouver spawned road rage, parking-lot rage, lineup rage and, in the entertainment district on downtown Granville Street, good, old drunken rage that led to bloody violence every night of the week. The violent crime was peculiarly stomach-turning. Newspaper stories about a pig farmer who murdered dozens of prostitutes included such nauseating details about his killings that the papers warned their more squeamish readers to skip them. The media gave us splashy yarns about Indo-Canadian men who murdered their wives in grotesque ways; a gang of youths who used bottles, bars, and the club lock for a car's steering wheel to kill a Filipino teenager; and nightclub bouncers who kept unruly customers in line by beating them to death. Vancouver's crime rate may have been no worse than Halifax's but, if you read the morning papers there, the violent crimes were more nightmarish. Who wants to be confronted by all that hate, horror, and sadism before breakfast?

After a rare blizzard destroyed three thousand trees in Vancouver's world-renowned Stanley Park, the local moaning and wailing suggested the city was a bit of a crybaby. For anyone who'd seen what Hurricane Juan did to Halifax – it felled some 60,000 trees in Point Pleasant Park alone – these lamentations were laughable. The damage to Stanley Park amounted to not a catastrophe but a mess. A natural mess. Big winds cull forests. They crack, uproot, prune, and topple weak trees. Others spring up. Life goes on. Stanley Park goes on.

Estimates put the cost of repairs at $4 million, but Vancouverites were so eager to nurse their dear old Stanley Park back to health that the restoration fund shot way past that. During a *Global News* telethon, businesses and individuals shelled out the first million. Billionaire Jimmy Pattison matched that, and pretty soon the non-government donations totalled $4.7 million. The province promised another $2 million, and Prime Minister Stephen Harper's suddenly greener-than-thou feds kicked in a further $2 million. The chairman of the parks board said all this made him "ecstatic." No doubt. The dreadful wind had turned into a wonderful windfall. He probably prayed that, every few years, another storm would blow over three thousand trees.

Not everyone saw the fund-raising story as heart-warming. Fretting in the *Vancouver Sun* about the city's booming population of homeless, one Marjorie Weir complained about "the raising of millions for trees lying on the ground, but nothing for people in the same position." Those who work among Vancouver street people believed half were mentally ill, and a participant in the Pender Harbour chat room said, "It bothers me that we're willing to let these people try to survive like feral animals while we get all worried about trees in a fucking park."

If it was out of the goodness of their hearts that many safe, comfy Vancouverites wanted to see the homeless off the streets, others had more hard-boiled reasons. The Winter Olympics in 2010 would attract to Vancouver tens of thousands of tourists and, as another Pender Harbour chatterer succinctly explained, "When you have insane, dirty, urine-soaked people trying to beg off the tourists, it doesn't get you a lot of repeat business."

Looking at a map of B.C., with its islands, inlets, and total coastline of roughly 16,000 miles, you'd think that leading out of Vancouver there'd be hour after hour of scenic coastal drives, but there aren't. From Halifax, you can drive pretty much beside the Atlantic Ocean all the way to Yarmouth or the Cabot Trail, and reach the Northumberland Shore in well under two hours. All along these routes you find beaches and seaside picnic parks.

But the mountains severely limit coastal driving near Vancouver. If you don't mind feeling boulders may bounce down from the cliffs above you and mash your car and everyone in it or, in winter, braving conditions so treacherous not even four-wheel-drive can save you from disaster, you may find some seaside scenery north of Vancouver on the road to Whistler. Going south on the main highway to the U.S. there's scarcely a glimpse of the ocean. The best coastal drives anywhere near Vancouver are on islands, and reaching them means studying ferry schedules, driving to docks, and lining up to board, both going and coming. I'd rather nip out to Crystal Crescent, Lawrencetown, Queensland, or any one of a dozen other beaches within ninety minutes of Halifax.

The mountains that dominate the northern skyline of Vancouver are undoubtedly beautiful, but also cold and forbidding. More and more, I remembered the barns and old farmhouses, and the green and rolling hills of Antigonish County. They were friendly. So were the orchards, dike lands, grazing cattle, and muddy tidal rivers of the Annapolis Valley. If I returned for a visit, would they whisper, "Welcome home, stranger, it's been a long time"?

By March of 2007, six months after settling in Vancouver for the rest of my life, I knew it was just too fast, noisy, pushy, and competitive for me. It had too many screaming sirens, too many people sleeping or shouting in streets and lanes, too many cars and trucks roaring through darkness and rain, and too many edgy people lining up, elbows high and tempers short, to buy everything from brunches to houses. Vancouver confirmed for me what I'd only begun to suspect after an earlier dash in and out of Toronto: I was no longer a big-city kind of guy. I was a small-city kind of guy and now, with Penny, Annabel, and Gabe, I would head a long way back east, all the way home to Halifax.

11

Home At Last

During the first March after we'd moved to Vancouver, I was already Googling Halifax real estate ads, and spotted a duplex that looked promising. Annabel instantly flew across Canada to inspect that one property. Then she phoned us. Yes, she said, this might just be the right home for all of us. Without having seen it, Penny and I joined her as partners in its purchase. By late April, with the four of us in one car, all our furniture following in a mover's van, and the delicate yellow-green of opening buds spreading throughout hardwoods all across the country, we drove down to our new home in old Halifax.

It was on Second Street, just one house away from Armcrescent East Drive. This was the very neighbourhood in which, thirty-six years and fourteen different dwellings before, Russell Harrington, the president of Nova Scotia Light and Power, had so warmly recommended we buy a house. If we'd followed his advice and stayed put, the money we'd have saved, by not having to pay inspectors, lawyers, moving companies, and real estate agents, would have been enough for Penny and me to have taken a luxury cruise around the world, with regular excursions into intriguing cities, preferably small.

Even after all those years, the neighbourhood was everything Harrington had said it was: a quiet, convenient pocket of the city, full of leafy trees, lush blossoms, helpful and generous adults, and good little boys and girls. With a two-bedroom apartment downstairs for us, a three-bedroom apartment on two upper floors for Annabel and Gabe, who was now five, and a big dry basement for everybody, the duplex would be our happy home for nine years. In no other dwelling did Penny and I ever stay that long. We were there pretty well throughout our seventies and into our eighties.

Gabe breezed through every grade of the nearby Sir Charles Tupper Elementary School. Back in the 1970s, when we lived on York Street, both his mother and Uncle Max had gone there, too. Its reputation was now so high among young parents that real estate ads habitually called the district "Tupperville." Remembering how bored, fearful, and miserable I felt during much of my time at grade school in Toronto, Gabe's never-ending happiness at Sir Charles Tupper astounded me. How could any boy possibly be so sunny for so long about any school? Half the schoolyard was a wide strip of grass, and the building, pinkish-beige for a while and then creamy, looked more inviting than any other public school in the city. Since Annabel was working downtown, Penny went to Tupper at mid-afternoon every weekday to join dozens of mothers in their thirties and forties, and two or three fathers, while they all waited together for a double door to open, and scores of kids, including Gabe, to burst outside.

One Wednesday afternoon in mid-October, I took over from Penny. A day to remember, full of sunshine and fall. Hardwoods encircled the school with high splashes of scarlet, orange, gold, bronze, and purple. The occasional leaf descended on a whisper of wind, and the joking, gossiping, and storytelling of the women sounded like a celebration of peace and contentment. Here was I then, the old man and the sea, a sea of mothers, waiting for his seven-year-old grandson to race out and give him a hug, and I was thinking, "We're Canadians and, my God, we're just the luckiest people on Earth."

The captain of *Ocean Watch*, a 64-foot, 44-ton, steel-hulled cutter, was my friend Mark Schrader, and on September 8, 2009, he e-mailed me that he and his crew expected to sail her into Halifax Harbour in about one week hence. Since May 31 they had sailed more than eight thousand miles, from Seattle up the British Columbia coast, around Alaska, eastward across the Arctic Circle twice, and then south into hair-raising storms on the Labrador Sea. Spread up and down on their white mainsail was a bright blue map of North and South America. For *Ocean Watch*, having reached Halifax, was well on her way to becoming the first sailboat ever to circumnavigate both continents during one voyage. The name of this remarkable mission was Around the Americas.

So far, *Ocean Watch* had sailed for less than a third

of the nearly 29,000 miles of their complete route, for only three and a half of the thirteen months that the historic voyage would take, and into just a dozen of the fifty-four ports in thirteen countries where she'd drop anchor. With the Northwest Passage under their belt, Mark and his crew now had four months of sailing time to contemplate the coming horrors of Cape Horn.

Around the Americas had a purpose beyond adventure. Its backers included Mark's friend, David Rockefeller Jr., and Sailors for the Sea. That's an organization Rockefeller co-founded to inspire his fellow pleasure-boaters to help restore the health of the oceans. The Pacific Science Center in Seattle contributed science and education programs to the expedition, and the University of Washington supplied a variety of essential analytical equipment. Scientists went aboard to measure atmospheric and ocean conditions under sail. Educators disembarked to explain ocean sciences at docksides, schools, and lecture halls, and to express *Ocean Watch*'s plea to the world: Save Our Seas.

They're under attack and, as the cartoon character Pogo said way back in 1972, "We have met the enemy and he is us." We overfish the oceans disastrously. We clog and poison them with plastic and chemical garbage. We accelerate the climate change that causes them not only to rise, but to get warmer, more acidic, and decidedly less friendly to life. The Great Barrier Reef of Australia is the mightiest coral reef in the world but, owing mostly to human activity, it's shrinking so fast that Dr. Nancy Knowlton, a marine scientist at the Smithsonian Institution in Washington, warned, "The entire world needs to act if we want the Great Barrier Reef to survive for our children and grandchildren."

About the cause behind the wind carrying *Ocean Watch* around two continents, Mark's message was even more urgent: "Nothing less than the survival of the oceans – and ultimately the human race – is at stake."

He and his wife Michele, the oldest daughter of Penny's sister Wendy, lived not far from the horse business that Wendy had founded in Stanwood, Washington. The home of Wendy and her husband Vincent was there on the farm, and their four children, daughters all, grew up knowing that home is not only where the heart is, but where the horses are. Mark, meanwhile, was the handiest handyman I'd ever known. Since I was a manually challenged literary chap who called a plumber whenever a faucet leaked, he struck me as a living miracle. Tanned, fit, and bearded, he worked out of an office and workshop in one of the cavernous and barn-like structures on the horse farm. He expertly wielded all manner of power tools, and operated tractors, dump trucks, bulldozers, and front-end loaders to build entire houses from their sewer pipes up to their chimney caps.

If Mark felt fine wearing a hard-hat, steel-toed boots, denim shirt, and maybe flame-resistant overalls, he felt even better while snug in the tough, warm, windproof, and water-resistant jackets and trousers of a man in a sailboat facing murderous weather off Antarctica. As a young buck in 1982-83 that's exactly what Mark did. He faced murderous weather off Antarctica. Throughout all the decades I saw myself as a sailor I never sailed anywhere past sundown or beyond the sight of land. I was sort of a Sunday afternoon sea dog. But Mark sailed around the world – alone – and not once but twice. He was the first American ever to do it while passing Cape Horn, the Cape of Good Hope, and the southernmost capes of Australia, Tasmania, and New Zealand.

It wasn't until a quarter-century later that Mark brought *Ocean Watch* up to the wide pier at Bishop's Landing on Lower Water Street. Michele flew from Seattle to Halifax to be with him for the first time in nearly four months. With her came her sister Stephanie, who would one day manage the family horse business, and Stephanie's friend from Seattle, Dan O'Connor. Shortly after *Ocean Watch* tied up opposite the shops at the landing, and the loving hugs of reunion had begun to give way to Mark's first discussions with curious and admiring yacht lovers from Halifax, Dan placed on the pier a set of speakers. Low and lilting music floated on the summer breeze, and he and Stephanie gracefully danced beside the rich blue of the harbour. The sun shone benignly on everything in sight and, cornball that I am, I couldn't help remembering lines by nineteenth-century poet Robert Browning: "God's in his heaven – All's right with the world!"

Owing to the population and potential media interest in Halifax, Mark's expedition ranked it, along with New York, Boston, Rio de Janeiro, Valparaiso, and Lima, as a class-A port of call. For two and a half centuries Halifax had esteemed bold sailors who braved dangerous waters on far oceans for good reasons, and I now counted on it to treat Mark and his crew as class-A heroes. And so it did.

"A capacity crowd for our presentation at the excellent Maritime Museum of the Atlantic showed us a humbling welcome," Herb McCormick, one of the crew, wrote in his book, *One Island, One Ocean* (2011).

He and onboard educator Zeta Strickland talked to classes at Sir Charles Tupper School about the Around the Americas adventure, ocean sciences, and the threats to the world's coastal and high seas. Only three years before, when Gabe was four, Mark had invited him to sit beside him while he drove a bulldozer around the horse farm in Stanwood and that, for the little boy, had been better than heaven. Now, still only seven and in grade two, he stood up before his classmates and formally introduced them to Captain Mark.

The night before *Ocean Watch* sailed past Point Pleasant Park, out to sea, and off to Boston, Annabel invited Mark and his crew to a farewell party in her apartment above ours on Second Street. Michele, Stephanie, Dan, Penny, and I were there, too, and it was as companionable a little gathering as I can ever remember being lucky enough to attend.

Aside from Mark, the guests of honour were Zeta Strickland, the onboard educator from the Pacific Science Center; Herb McCormick, the former editor of *Cruising World* magazine and yachting correspondent for *The New York Times*; David Thoreson, a renowned photographer and filmmaker, and the first American to sail through the Northwest Passage in both directions; and Mark's first mate, Dave Logan. A Seattle cabinet-maker and lifelong sailor, Logan was quiet, handy, multi-talented and, in Mark's eyes, indispensable to the success of *Ocean Watch*'s dangerous and unprecedented voyage.

Speaking of "dangerous," gale-force winds and wild, mountainous waves bullied and banged *Ocean Watch* for several days as she rampaged south on the Labrador Sea. Exhausted crew napped only after strapping themselves into their bunks. Controlling the cutter left them so desperately busy that for meals they could only shove crackers and cheese into their mouths.

"The 'liquid Himalayas' continued to build and grow," McCormick remembered in *One Island, One Ocean,* "and at one stage, in a 45-knot gust of wind, *Ocean Watch* flew down the face of a monster – we estimated that the biggest waves were cresting at a good 30 feet – at a best-ever speed of 17 knots. Off to leeward we were shocked to see what a fulmar looks like – flying backward." Skidding down sideways on such waves "in a 64-foot steel missile," he continued, "had been an interesting experience. It was one we didn't hope to repeat."

Right. Mark told me that those days and nights on the Labrador Sea were among the most unnerving he had ever spent on the oceans of the world. But some good news did emerge from the ordeal. *Ocean Watch* had proved herself as a superb performer in the dirtiest weather.

Just before *Ocean Watch* sailed out of our Halifax lives, the first copies of the best book I ever wrote arrived from my publisher in Toronto. It was *Page Fright: Foibles and Fetishes of Famous Writers.* I gave a copy to Mark, and off it went, bound for Seattle, via Cape Horn. Two months later he told me by e-mail, "We're slowly making our way around the enormous northeastern bulge of South America ... I haven't had much time for reading but after Puerto Rico our pace relaxed a little and I was able to pick up *Page Fright.* Herb and Dave Logan noticed me smiling while reading it, then chuckling to myself, and then laughing out loud. This morning they both have their noses in your book, both smiling. We all agreed, this is a great read."

Advice to writers who crave praise for their latest book: plant a copy among the crew of an ocean-going sailboat that's far offshore with no other publications on board except navigation charts. The last pages of *One Island, One Ocean* acknowledge the scores of organizations, businesses, and friends that backed Around the Americas. One long list of individuals from several countries begins splendidly: "During our circumnavigation of the Americas, we enjoyed remarkable hospitality and/or advice and support from the Bruce family (Harry, Penny, Annabel, and Gabe)."

Intensive research on Google reveals that Mark, as the spouse of my wife's niece, is my "co-nephew-in-law." I am proud to declare myself the only resident of the great little city of Halifax who can boast a co-nephew-in-law who sailed twice around the world alone, and commanded the first continuous circumnavigation by sail of both North and South America. He did that clockwise. Now, a decade later, he and his allies are raising funds to do it counterclockwise. Is there no stopping the man?

Back when we were very young, we saw a movie called *The Incredible Shrinking Man*, but now that we are pretty old we realize we're members of The Incredible Growing Family. In Halifax, it includes one son, one daughter, one daughter-in-law, one son-in-law, one grandson, one granddaughter, one grandson-in-law, one great-granddaughter, and two great-grandsons. We regularly see every one of them.

In Toronto, we have a granddaughter, grandson-in-law, great-grandson, and great-granddaughter. Some or all of them come down home for a week or so every summer, and the parents in this Upper Canadian branch of the family are pondering their chances of settling here for good.

Then there's the Los Angeles branch. That's our younger son Max and his partner Tony. They visit us every Christmas, without fail, for at least a week.

And come the next jolly yuletide season, I'll be thinking about the whole of this incredible growing family when I steal from Charles Dickens the immortal wish of Tiny Tim: "A Merry Christmas to us all; and God bless us all, every one." And who could ask for anything more?

But if it weren't for the miracle that a surgical team at the Halifax Infirmary pulled off for me on September 10, 2019, I doubt I'd have survived long enough to wish for any such thing. I'd merely be a deceased patriarch. Back in December of 2018, tests and consultations with doctors and nurses had led to my being approved for a TAVI. That stands for Transcatheter Aortic Valve Insertion. The aortic valve controls the flow of oxygen-rich blood from your left ventricle out to your aorta, which is your biggest artery. The aorta then channels the blood to other arteries, and they send it on to your brain, muscles, and everything else in your body.

If you allow the piston assembly of your car engine to degenerate until it breaks down, you'll have to have a new one installed. Well, I had spent several decades gobbling so much salty, sugary, and fatty food, guzzling so much gin, rum, and whisky, and smoking so many tens of thousands of cigarettes that my aortic artery had degenerated until it was about to break down. And I was only eighty-four. I had to get a new one installed. It would be fashioned from the heart tissue of some poor pig.

After learning I was in line for a TAVI, I had to wait for it for no fewer than nine months. Meanwhile, slowly but relentlessly, I grew feebler, dizzier, and shorter of breath. My walking deteriorated until I could do little more than drag myself around our condo. I conked out regularly while seated at my desk, and grew so short of breath I could not sleep at night. Pulling on my socks left me gasping for air as though I'd just crossed the finish line at a marathon.

Since the longer a TAVI "wait time" lasts the greater the risk that, first, the operation will be less effective than it should be and, second, the recovery will take longer, I was not happy to learn via Google that the "median total wait time" in Ontario was not nine months, but three and a half. Claiming even that was too long, an outfit called Heart Valve Voice Canada asserted that aortic valve disease "only worsens without appropriate treatment; 50 percent of patients will likely die within two years."

And then, at last, came my time under the lights. I arrived at the Halifax Infirmary mid-morning, and early that afternoon, a couple of bafflingly chirpy nurses rolled me face up on a gurney to an anesthetist. A short, amiable, and dynamic middle-aged woman, she pushed her face close to mine and loudly enunciated brief instructions.

The next thing I knew, or half-knew, Penny was smiling beside me. I was groggy, and mumbled, "What seems to be the problem?" No problem. Opening and closing beautifully inside my chest was my new aortic valve. Thanks to what American conservatives revile as "socialized medicine," it cost me nothing. The price for anyone without medical insurance in the U.S. would have been upwards of $60,000 (that's $80,000 Canadian).

For reasons known only to surgeons, a TAVI is not an operation but a "procedure." Following surgical trials little more than a decade ago, TAVIs have installed aortic valves in close to half a million people. Before TAVIs, no one got a new valve without undergoing open-heart surgery. That meant stopping the heart, hooking the patient up to a heart-lung machine, splitting the breast bone open with a saw and, with the heart and its valves thus exposed, completing the installation. This took up to six hours, and the patient then had to remain in hospital for a week or even two. For patients like me, weakened by age and disease, a TAVI is far better. It's not only less exhausting and intrusive, but quicker and safer.

Compressed, my new valve was inflatable, like a balloon. To install it, the surgical team attached it to the end of a catheter (a pencil-sized tube); cut slits in my groin, one on each side of my genitals; then stuck the catheter into one of the slits; and, using three-dimensional X-ray apparatus to help guide the delivery, forced it all the way up through a major artery to the diseased valve. My tiny, new, and life-extending gadget was now inflated and, shoving the rotten one aside, it snugly took its place.

If the procedure had not turned out as it did, I'd have had trouble believing it was even possible. But the very next day, while breathing normally for the first time in a year, I gently walked several laps around a small circle of corridors outside my room in the Infirmary. And the day after that, Penny drove me home. For the first time, I fully understood the daily heroism of hospital staff in what I had finally recognized as my hometown.

Standing in a balmy breeze out on the balcony of our eleventh-floor condo near Windsor and North streets, I can see a deep blue swath of the harbour, the ferries and big ships going about their business, the cars and trucks pushing both ways on the new bridge off to the north and the old bridge straight ahead in the east, and, in the south, the high-rises and higher-rises near the downtown waterfront, the skyscraping cranes, the green mound of Citadel Hill, and, if I lean far enough out over the railing, the horizon of the far ocean. I'm eighty-six. I've been here four years, and somehow that whole scene – including even the ambulances, fire engines, and police cars that scream up and down Robie Street – has gradually been bringing into focus why I've come to love Halifax.

It's the only city in Canada where you'll find, in the downtown business district, the residence of twenty-six horses. They belong to the Junior Bengal Lancers where, over the past eighty-four years, thousands of the children of Halifax have gotten together with "The Horses of Halifax." The club's headquarters, barn, paddock, and riding circles are all at 1690 Bell Road, and that's only a short canter from Citadel Hill in one direction and The Public Gardens in another.

After seeing the movie *The Lives of a Bengal Lancer* (1935), local horse-lover M.B. "Dick" Zwicker founded the club as a way to teach city children to love, ride, and care for horses. Wearing red tunics, khaki jodhpurs, white gloves, and pith helmets, and carrying lances with pennants, a team of sixteen riders and horses quickly mastered a junior version of the RCMP Musical Ride. They wowed audiences not only here but in Toronto and Boston, and young Lancers still ride the ride just as musically as ever. And just as reliably as ever, horses sidle over from the paddock to the fence beside the Bell Road sidewalk to meet the pedestrians who stop to pat them lovingly, and sometimes feed them an apple or two.

If the smell of grass comforts horses, these are supremely content. For no other city in Canada grows so much grass mere steps away from its downtown eateries and hotels, apartment towers and cement mixers, buses and trucks, bars and bustle, honks and hustle, and banks and businesses. Greenbacks are cheek by jowl with greenery here, and the oldest city park in Canada, the Commons, is only a few hundred yards from City Hall. Yet the Commons offers courts for tennis and basketball, diamonds for baseball, softball, and lob-ball, fields for football, soccer, and cricket, and an outdoor oval four hundred metres long for ice-skating in winter and inline skating in summer. Then there's the Commons skatepark. That's an arrangement of ramps, half-pipes, funboxes, and other concrete challenges for aggressive young tricksters on skateboards, scooters, bikes, and inline skates.

At a softball diamond in the Commons a mere sixty-seven years ago – before I'd ever even seen a TV set – I was a pitcher during a game between teams of RCN officer-cadets. In the bottom of the last inning,

I preserved a victory for our side when, unassisted, I turned what looked like a sure hit by the enemy into a triple play, thereby ending the game. (How did I do this? Never mind. It's too complicated to explain.) That diamond today is exactly where it was then.

Close by, and even further downtown, looms Citadel Hill. Fort George, magnificently restored, sprawls all over the peak. It's one of the most popular National Historic Sites in the country and stays open year-round. Bristling with cannons and surrounded by dry moats, the fort echoes to the sounds of the 78th Highlanders as they quick-march and present arms in their nineteenth-century uniforms.

Down the long, steep, grassy slopes that drop away from the fort, children roll over and over, screaming with delight. Sunbathers stretch out and bake at a comfortable angle. Picnickers get together under the odd shady tree and, high above the whole scene, a flashy assortment of signal flags and national flags snaps and flutters in the summer breeze. The grass on the slopes somehow stays deep green right up until snow falls. Before long, children and whole families will show up with their sleds, sleighs, toboggans, and slide sheets. If you walk just a quarter-mile down Duke Street from the east side of Citadel Hill, you cross the very heart of the downtown and arrive at the harbour. This stroll might take you all of five minutes.

Flanked by Sackville Street and Bell Road, with the hill looming in the background, the Garrison Grounds serves as a natural amphitheatre for audiences of anywhere up to 30,000 people. The crowds show up for rock concerts, music festivals, the RCMP Musical Ride, and all manner of events that require the blossoming of big white tents. Are there no gatherings here this week or next? No matter. The green grass grows all around, all around.

On the north side of Sackville Street, and no further west of the Garrison Grounds than you could throw a baseball, there's another field where the green grass grows. This is the Wanderers Grounds where, off and on during the past 140 years or so, teams have competed at baseball, cricket, rugby, soccer, high school football, track and field, and lawn bowling. None other than Babe Ruth showed up here in the summer of 1942. The main event was a game between navy teams but, while a Halifax pitcher threw the ball over home plate, Ruth, who was forty-two and seven years retired, whacked it into the stands for boys to catch.

These days, the darling among Wanderers Grounds sports is not amateur baseball but the city's first professional soccer team, none other than – yessiree, ladeez and gennulmen – the one and only Halifax Wanderers! They have a snappy, new, 6,000-seat stadium on the historic grounds, a rabid gang of fans to gobble up tickets, and, again, not artificial turf to play upon but the green, green grass of home.

Directly across Sackville Street lies the finest example in North America of public gardens arranged in the formal style that was so popular in Victorian England. Established in 1874, when Her Majesty turned fifty-five and her favourite prime minister, Benjamin Disraeli, returned to power, The Public Gardens of Halifax completely fills a big city block. It's calm, hushed, and intimate, yet spectacular. Wide, straight, gravel paths and narrow, curved pathways make their way under voluminous elms; among tropical plants, exotic foliage, and more than 140 tree species; past extravagant beds of blossoms set against flawless lawns; and around a little *Titanic* afloat on a wide pond. The ship shares the pond with dozens of smug-looking ducks. From time to time, swans and rotund geese have hung out around the nearby stream. At the main entrance stands the biggest cast-iron gate I've ever seen. Black, regal, and highly ornate, it's sixteen feet high and twenty-one wide. Just inside, two pretty footbridges lead visitors over a gurgling brook, and on toward the classic Victorian bandstand at the heart of the park. Painted in bright primary colours and encrusted with the most elaborate gingerbread, this gazebo is as Victorian as Gilbert and Sullivan. It's a beloved working antique. Fat vases rise from flower beds that encircle it. Scattered elsewhere are statues of a Boer War rifleman and ancient Rome's three goddesses of nature, as well as lofty bronze fountains, one with water babies riding sea serpents around its base.

On a sunny afternoon last summer we visited the canteen there to buy waffle cones jammed with gobs of ice cream that tasted of sea salt, caramel, and chocolate chips. Seated on a bench under a shady tree, we bit off mouthfuls, sucked them back, and marvelled that this was beyond doubt the most delicious ice cream we'd ever tasted anywhere. A fanfare, please! Jazz from the 1940s burst forth from speakers near the bandstand. It sounded like the Count Basie Orchestra. Four middle-aged couples, who had surely been taking jitterbug lessons, jumped up, and charged into a joyful session of rhythmic bouncing, twirling, and swinging. We hadn't seen such jitterbugging in sixty years, and the scene was a beautiful gift. We were well into our eighties, and it was only now that I understood The Public Gardens would always have a gift ready for us.

Just across Spring Garden Road, here in New Scotland, a statue of the bard of old Scotland, Robert Burns, strikes a noble pose. Behind his back there's yet another big patch of downtown grass. Victoria Park stretches southward for an entire block. On the eastern side, there's a bust of Sir Walter Scott, whose best historical novels have for two centuries remained classics of both Scottish and English literature. In the southern end, a monument memorializes Sir William Alexander. He was a Scottish poet and writer of rhyming tragedies, a favourite in the royal courts of both James I and Charles I, and a would-be colonizer of Nova Scotia. In 1629, he installed some seventy Scots in the future Annapolis Royal, but only three years later a treaty restored French control of the neighbourhood. The Scots vanished. It was nevertheless Sir William's tiny, fleeting settlement that gave Nova Scotia its name, flag, and coat-of-arms.

Surrounded by racketing traffic, Victoria Park is mysteriously soothing. It could not be in plainer sight, yet its path-side benches, its green and gentle slopes, and the shadows that the tall graceful hardwoods cast, these all conspire to give it a feeling of secrecy. It's special. It's the only park in Canada, and maybe in the world, that commemorates not one, not two, but three writers with Scottish surnames. I'm a writer. I'm a Bruce. How could I not like Victoria Park?

12

Blithe Spirits!

Halifax is daffodils and cannons, fog and ironstone, kilts and gulls, kites and lobster rolls, donairs and Cape Islanders, old spires and new penthouses, your own backyard and the big shipyard, the "trendy North End" and the poodles in the park, Joe Howe in bronze and the *Titanic* in miniature, a broken man on a Halifax pier and Oscar Wilde at the Waverley Inn. Halifax is helicopters that cruise back and forth over the ocean and the basin, sailboats that flit around monster container ships like flies around a rhinoceros, and clattering boxcars that go down to the sea on rails. It's also just taking your lover on a hot summer day to the sun-blasted roof of our gorgeous downtown library. Sit at a table under a parasol. Sip iced coffee and, once again, admire one of the deepest, bluest, and shapeliest harbours in the world.

While I can't possibly record all the scenes, sounds, and revelations that swim in my head to make me feel so good about Halifax these days, a certain visit by the flagship of the Cunard Line, *Queen Mary II*, would certainly be high on the list. She's the tallest, longest, widest, strongest, and fastest ocean liner ever built. In 1840 her ancestor, *Britannia*, made the first transatlantic crossing of a ship under steam power alone. That led to the founding by her builder, Halifax-born Samuel Cunard, of the first back-and-forth, scheduled service across the Atlantic. It was to celebrate the 175th anniversary of that historic voyage that *Queen Mary II* repeated it on July 10, 2015.

That evening, Penny and I were at the Halifax Jazz Festival hard by the boardwalk when the Voice of Cuba Orchestra launched a swinging-like-crazy concert. Just as the setting sun cast a pink glow over the whole harbour, *Queen Mary II* sprang a magnificent surprise. As though answering a curtain call, her surge-slicing bow magically emerged from the north, and then her whole length slid by – she's three times bigger than the *Titanic* was – and hundreds upon hundreds of her 2,600 passengers stood out on her decks to wave and wave at us.

Bound for Boston, she gave us a couple of deep-deep-down reverberating and majestic blasts. Pause. She did it again. All of us in the jazz crowd jumped up to applaud, and the Cuban orchestra began to harmonize with the supremely bass horns of the great ship to create a few seconds of the strangest and most gloriously funny music I have heard in all my eight decades. Only in Halifax, I thought, only on a soft summer night in Halifax. A city to dance in.

About the Author

Harry Bruce is the author of 14 previous books and – for them, his newspaper columns, and his magazine stories – has won a raft of awards and a couple of honourary degrees. He launched his career at the age of 20, no fewer than 66 years ago, and now holds the Lifetime Achievement Award of the Atlantic Journalism Awards organization. *The Concise Oxford Companion to Canadian Literature* calls him "an essayist of great charm and perception."

Books by Harry Bruce

The Short Happy Walks of Max MacPherson

Lifeline: The Story of the Atlantic Ferries and Coastal Boats

R.A.: The Story of R. A. Jodrey: Entrepreneur

Each Moment As It Flies

Movin' East

The Man and the Empire: Frank Sobey

Down Home: Notes of a Native Son

Maud: The Life of L.M. Montgomery

The Life of Frank Manning Covert: Corporate Navigator

The Pig That Flew: The Battle to Privatize Canadian National

An Illustrated History of Nova Scotia

Never Content: How Mavericks and Outsiders Made a Surprise Winner of Maritime Life

Tall Ships: An Odyssey

Page Fright: Foibles and Fetishes of Famous Writers

Praise for *Page Fright: Foibles and Fetishes of Famous Writers*

Tells more about the creative process than a dozen academic textbooks, and makes for delightful browsing.
— Edward O. Wilson, biologist and twice winner of a Pulitzer Prize

A gem of a book for writers and wannabe writers alike.
— National Post

An essential book. It's invaluable for any writer facing deadlines, the absence of sobriety, writer's block, an unexpected outbreak of leprosy, or any of the myriad excuses we scribblers use to postpone the agonizing ecstasy of completing our works. Buy it. Read it. And stop procrastinating.
— Peter C. Newman

Bruce gives readers much to savour. You can start anywhere and find something to inspire and fascinate.
— Ottawa Citizen

This is a splendid feast of literary lore, wonderfully readable and quite amazingly comprehensive.
— Robert Fulford

An utterly fascinating, sometimes downright scary, exhaustively researched compendium of writer's lifestyles – their superstitions, their foibles, their train wrecks and their triumphs. What a crew!"
— Andreas Schroeder

Bruce writes effortlessly, and readers are engaged before they know it – we are obviously in the hands of a master.
— Hamilton Spectator